MEERA MAJITHIA is a specialist ~~|~~ planner. She works closely with coup~~|~~ helping them to realise their vision of the winning wedding professional, Meera has featured widely in regional, national and international press and was one of the first in her industry to create an online wedding planning platform for brides.

She was bitten by the wedding planning bug at age 16, when she worked at one of the UK's first specialist Indian wedding planning companies. After graduating in Management at undergraduate level and completing a Masters in Journalism, Meera combined her skillset and launched a wedding planning company. Carriages Weddings & Events was to be a wedding planning company with a difference, priding itself on offering beautiful, meaningful experiences. The one thing that all of Meera's weddings have in common is that they are each unique to the couple at hand and to their story. This speaks to Meera's core belief – that weddings should be personality-led, as originality never goes out of style.

In her spare time, Meera presents on the radio and frequently enjoys putting her vegan baking skills to the test.

PLANNED *to* PERFECTION

A MODERN APPROACH TO WEDDING PLANNING
FOR THE INDIAN & INTERFAITH BRIDE

Meera Majithia

SilverWood

Published in 2020 by SilverWood Books

SilverWood Books Ltd
14 Small Street, Bristol, BS1 1DE, United Kingdom
www.silverwoodbooks.co.uk

ISBN 978-1-80042-033-5 (paperback)
ISBN 978-1-80042-034-2 (ebook)

British Library Cataloguing in Publication Data
A CIP catalogue record for this book is
available from the British Library

Page design and typesetting by SilverWood Books

For my mum and dad, for their constant encouragement and support. And for my couples, for allowing me to have the most incredible job in the world.

Contents

Introduction

If you've grown up on a diet of Jane Austen classics, Bollywood romances or Disney fairy tales, then you'll be very familiar with the idea of a happily ever after, which usually starts with a *wedding*. For centuries, weddings have been depicted as a magical, ground-breaking life event – and rightly so! Your marriage begins on this very wedding day, which means it's only right that everything is as perfect as can be. And trust me, perfect weddings do exist. But for many brides and grooms, the pressure of achieving this perfection can be too much. Some don't know where to start, some don't have the time and some simply struggle to bring their vision to life – which is where professionals like me come in.

I live for creating beautiful, meaningful wedding experiences and helping brides and grooms just like you plan the wedding of their dreams. The rush of excitement I feel when the nuptials arrive is amazing, but that warm, fuzzy feeling I get from seeing how happy my couples look on their big day is second to none. I wake up every day feeling grateful that I have one of the most incredible jobs on the planet – I really do!

With a lot of hard work and a sprinkling of luck, I've seen my company grow into something I'd only ever dreamed of. Carriages Weddings & Events was born in 2015 and offers traditional wedding planning and coordination services. Since then, my passion for the industry and my clients has seen me diversify and add various other strands to the business, including Virtual Wedding Planning and working as an Asian Wedding Consultant. I also launched my private members-only wedding planning club, *Planned To Perfection*, which allows me to help couples all over the world with their wedding journey as their Bridal Coach, at a fraction of the cost of hiring a planner.

While everyone dreams of having an Instagram-worthy wedding, it's no secret that each of you will be working to a different budget (we'll come back to this later), and the reason for writing this book was to ensure that expert industry advice is available to literally *everyone*. The idea of being an expert at doing something I love still feels quite surreal, but over the years I've had the incredible opportunity to be featured in local and national press, won multiple awards and worked at some highly prestigious venues.

You might be wondering how I became Wedding Planner-in-Chief. Well, let's just say it was quite a lengthy process that started off with me volunteering for one of the UK's first Asian wedding planning companies at the age of sixteen and shadowing my dad who to this day organises one of Leicester's largest religious festivals. Of course, I'm actually in charge of the festival now! And so, eleven years after my first wedding planning stint I found my true calling and have never looked back since. In a nutshell, this is me and this is why I wrote this book. I'm passionate about the work that I do and want to help you plan the wedding you've not only been dreaming of, but the wedding you truly deserve!

So, I hope you're ready to go on this journey with me…

I've started off this book by introducing you to a couple who, despite their frosty first meeting, are getting ready to plan their own wedding. We'll follow their journey right up to their wedding day and hopefully their experience will help you better understand and sympathise with some of the uncertainties and challenges that arise during the planning process.

Sometimes it's far easier to see something from a bird's-eye perspective and this is how I intend for you to relate to Rishi and Selena's story. The book is structured in three parts, which reflect the three different stages you'll go through while planning your wedding. Here's a quick overview so that you know what to expect:

Part One

This is your guide from the moment you get engaged. It's not always easy navigating through the countless thoughts flowing in and out of your mind. If you combine this with a never-ending list of questions from friends, family members and well-wishers then you'll understand why focusing on your mindset during this time is important. Your attitude, emotions and actions need to be focused on achieving your end goal while feeling happy.

Part Two

In this section, we'll dive into some of the broader wedding planning topics so that you have a thorough understanding of the basics before you start to put together the finer details. We'll specifically be looking at how you manage your time, budget and distractions, and I'll be revealing my top tips on how you can secure good quality suppliers.

Part Three

These are your essential tips as you get into the nitty-gritty stages of planning. We'll focus on your wedding venue, styling your event and putting together your event schedule. Reading and actioning the points in this last chapter are crucial if you wish to execute a successful event (which I know you do!).

My main advice for you right now is to read this book in chronological order first, despite how tempting it might be to skip to the back. The reason being, a lot of the things we'll be covering at the start of the book will lay the foundations for the later parts. Following your initial read, I have no doubt that you'll want to dive into certain sections more than others depending on where you are in the planning process, and this is completely normal. Complete the exercises as you go and you'll be on your way to planning your wedding like a pro. Just remember: this process is supposed to be enjoyable, and I'm going to be right by your side until the big day to cheer you on and make sure this is the case.

Let's get planning!

The First Meeting

June 2016
An old barn in the middle of nowhere

Rishi stared at the damp napkin that lay on the bar top in front of him and reread his scribbled notes for what felt like the hundredth time. He wasn't someone who usually needed notes to entertain a crowd – public speaking just seemed to come naturally to him. But the pressure of delivering the best man's speech was something else. It had to be funny but "clean" (there were lots of parents in the room, including his own), deep but not soppy, and precisely no longer than fifteen minutes – he was under strict instructions from the wedding planner.

He twisted his pen to a close and folded the napkin into his jacket pocket, signalling the bartender over. He smiled. Best man duties certainly came with their perks as the waiter unwillingly handed over two bottles of Grey Goose. No one was going to miss a bottle or two, and besides, he'd personally dropped all the alcohol at the venue the night before and knew there was plenty to last till sunrise. Rishi reached over and pulled the bottles towards his chest, using his opposite hand to stack up a couple of chunky glasses. He swung round feeling quite smug, when all of a sudden someone rushed in from behind causing him to lose balance. He watched in horror as both bottles smashed to the floor.

'Idiot,' he mumbled, as he crouched down, trying to wipe the liquid off his expensive shoes.

'Excuse me?'

He looked up. Staring down at him with a fierce scowl was one of the most beautiful faces he had ever seen.

'S…sorry, I thought you were one of the lads. Are you okay?'

'Fine!' she lied. The alcohol had splattered across the bottom of her designer dress and all over her favourite *and only* pair of Jimmy Choos. Even worse, the crash of the bottle meant they were now starting to turn heads.

'I'm not usually this clumsy,' he said.

She rolled her eyes.

Within seconds, the wedding planner came rushing in with two members of staff, a bucket, mop and a wet-floor sign, indicating for the two of them to move aside. The woman was more than grateful and rushed off to the ladies. Rishi stood alone feeling a little dumbstruck. He suddenly felt a flutter in his stomach, and knew it had nothing to do with the speech he was about to deliver.

Part One

Getting Started

You've most likely picked up this book because you've just got engaged or are at the start of your wedding planning journey (or perhaps somewhere in the middle) and are looking for some guidance. I've got experience in planning and executing multiple successful events, so I promise you, no matter which stage you're at, there are some golden nuggets in this book that are going to be incredibly valuable to you.

By the end of this section you will have figured out what your dream wedding *really* looks like and how to communicate this to your partner, friends, family or anyone who's going to help you plan the big day. You will also learn to cope with any stressful situations that may arise during the planning process. I'd secretly like to think that all my couples have a happy and drama-free journey, but we all know this isn't actually the case. That's why the start of this book focuses on mindset. Our mindset is important in every aspect of life and determines how we approach any situation, including planning a wedding. A large part of successful wedding planning comes down to how you cope with stress, which is why it's vital that you don't skip this section.

I know you've got this!

P.S. As you're reading away, don't forget to click a picture with your copy and tag @carriagesevents on your social profiles. I always love connecting with my brides and grooms so please do say hello.

The Proposal

June 2017

Exactly one year later in Santorini, Greece

'Selena Chauhan, I knew from that very first moment I laid eyes on you that I was going to marry you.'

'And what made you think I would agree to be *your* wife?'

'I could tell you were into me. You just didn't want to show it.'

She almost choked with a fit of laughter.

'Trust me, you don't want to know what I was thinking.'

Selena placed her glass of champagne on the table and slid her Ray-Ban sunglasses to the top of her head. She could get used to this view. In front of her was nothing but the open sea, and as the sun started to go down, it seemed to have taken the noise with it. There would be live music and lots of chatter coming from the nearby cobbled streets later as people headed out for drinks and dinner, but right now, all she could hear from their balcony was the crashing of the waves below. *And unfortunately the buzzing of their phones.*

It had been approximately twenty-four hours since Rishi had popped the question in what had since become her favourite place in the world. He had carefully constructed every part of the proposal to make sure it was nothing short of perfect. He began by leaving her a note in their room asking her to join him for dinner on the rooftop terrace. Turns out, he'd hired the entire terrace and filled the space with fairy lights and dozens of red roses. They had a five-course candlelit dinner, while enjoying a rendition of traditional Greek songs from a bouzouki player, followed by a few of her Bollywood favourites, which the musician had learned specifically for the evening. They laughed, danced and drank lots of wine before Rishi got down on one knee and asked her to be his wife – *with a blue box in his hand.*

Though they'd discussed telling their families the next day, she was too excited and immediately FaceTimed both sets of parents and her best friend, Tash, back home. Before they knew it, word had spread – which meant by the time they woke up the next morning, both of their phones were flooded with congratulatory messages and had not stopped pinging ever since. In all honesty, Selena was somewhat regretting not asking her family to keep the news to themselves. She was already being quizzed about where the wedding was going to take place, if they had a date in mind and if they'd booked a venue yet (of course they hadn't!).

She felt anxious at the thought of it all and wished she had a few weeks alone with Rishi on this dreamy island before they had to head back home to reality. It's not that she wasn't grateful for the love – she enjoyed a good party and couldn't wait to celebrate with everyone – but for now, she was determined to enjoy the next forty-eight hours in peace before having to think about anything else. She reached for her phone, flicked the off button and sank back into her chair. She was living the good life, at least for now…

Chapter One

You've Just Got Engaged. What's Next?

Congratulations on your engagement. If you haven't yet overindulged in cake and celebrated with a glass or two of champagne, what are you waiting for? You're going to be floating on clouds for at least the next few weeks, so enjoy this time. And remember, it's completely normal and acceptable to constantly find excuses to show off your engagement ring. You aren't the first bride to do this and you certainly won't be the last!

I want this warm/happy/exciting/magical feeling you're experiencing to last for a long time, which is why I've specifically written this section. The very first thing you need to do is process what has just happened. You have just agreed to marry the man or woman of your dreams, which is a pretty *big* deal. Take twenty-four hours, a few days or a few weeks if you need, to simply breathe, relax and soak it all in. Let's take Selena's story as an example. While sharing your good news with immediate family members is a must, it's important to remember that unless specifically instructed, they're going to be *very* excited and will start spreading the good news with others ASAP. If you're ready for this then go for it, but if not, take some time to think over what you're going to do next before you announce it to the world. I understand there's also a temptation to dive right into wedding planning, but try and resist the urge.

The purpose of this book is to help you every step of the way on your wedding journey. You may have friends, colleagues or family members who have shared their wedding planning approach with you, which is really great, but do not feel pressured into following the same route. As someone who has planned many, many weddings, I can tell you there is a clear structure (though sometimes we need to deviate from this a little) and it's best to stick to this approach, or else you're going to end up feeling overwhelmed.

Once you've fully celebrated your engagement and are ready to move on to the next stage you'll want to:

◊ Put together a provisional guest list highlighting your numbers.

◊ Make a rough note of the total amount of money you want to spend on your wedding.

◊ Pick a date (or a few, so you have some flexibility).

◊ Start thinking about your ideal location and venue.

These seem like really simple tasks, but you'll be surprised at how long it takes you to narrow these things down. For example, if you come from a religious family then you may need to liaise with a priest to check for any auspicious or suitable marriage dates. If you don't come from a religious family, you may still need to speak to both your and your partner's immediate families to avoid any potential schedule conflicts.

Wedding tip: Always be sure to cross-check the calendar to see if your potential wedding date clashes with any large sporting tournaments or global events. You probably don't want your guests to be glued to their phones throughout the ceremony so it's worth bearing this in mind.

What matters most?

The next step is to make a list of your three top wedding day priorities. For example, have you always dreamed of having an outdoor wedding? Is your main priority to ensure every single member of your family is in attendance?

Do you need to locate a venue that is practical for any elderly or disabled family members? These three things can be about absolutely anything. You may have dreamed your whole life about wearing a bespoke Sabyasachi dress, in which case you'll want to factor this into your overall budget. It's important for you and your partner to make separate lists to begin with so you can both identify what's important to you individually. Then go through this list together, and as a couple pick three things that stand out to you.

You might find that you and your partner have the exact same priorities, which is fantastic, or you might find that you want different things from the day, which is also completely okay. Marriages do after all involve compromise and this begins with your wedding day. Having to make a compromise doesn't mean that you're not going to get the day you always dreamed of. Instead, it shows the deep commitment and love you have for one another and the lengths you're willing to go to make each other happy. If you struggle to narrow down your list to three things, then pick two each. This seems fair, don't you think? Now, you'll want to write these out and keep them somewhere visible or keep them in a shared digital document that you can both easily access.

One of the key reasons for making the "what matters most" list is if you get stuck about any wedding-related decisions going forward, you can return to this list and ask yourself the question: does this align with our overall vision for the day and what we really want? If not, then you'll know that it's often something you can live without.

It's quite easy to get carried away and start focusing on the flavour of your cake or the types of flowers you want on display, but these things are going to come much later on down the line – unless of course flowers are a big part of your day (and in some instances they can be, which might mean that securing your dream florist is a priority). Every wedding is different, so it's always important to keep your priorities and ideas in mind when making any decisions. I know from past experience that the checklist below is a great guide to get you started. Work your way through the list in order and you'll stay on track with your planning.

◊ Purchase wedding insurance.

◊ Secure wedding venue.

◊ Contact wedding stationery provider to send out save the dates.

◊ Book an appointment with the registry office.

◊ Book celebrant or priest.

◊ Book photographer.

◊ Narrow down caterers and start booking in tastings.

◊ Finalise a stylist, florist and/or décor company.

◊ Book in a trial with your chosen make-up and/or hair stylist.

◊ Book DJ and/or band.

◊ Book accommodation (if required).

◊ Start scheduling cake tastings.

◊ Book transport.

◊ Book any other entertainment (photo booth, live instrumentalists etc).

Wedding tip: You may wish to have your save the dates professionally designed and printed. After all, this is the first glimpse people are going to get of your event. However, if you are looking for a budget-friendly option you could send the invitations out electronically, or possibly design them yourself using a free online design tool.

Pssst...I use Canva for a lot of my design work and it's brilliant. (I have no affiliation with the brand.)

Moving on, just remember that before you sign any contracts with your suppliers, you'll want to ask them some key questions to make sure they can provide everything you want and need, with no hidden terms or charges being brought forward at a later date. I have a list ready inside my private wedding community, so if you feel like taking the leap to sign up, then you'll be relieved to find that this task will have already been done for you. If not, I'd advise you to go into any meeting fully prepared with a list of written questions to be sure that you don't forget anything.

Now it may sound obvious, but you'll definitely need to keep a written record of all your correspondence. While a shiny new wedding notebook will be useful to accompany you on meetings, you'll probably want to create a digital folder to store important contracts and email correspondence. I use Dropbox and Google Drive, however you can use any other tool you prefer. The main thing is for you and your partner to have easy access to this at *all times* so you can cross-reference things whenever you need. If you remain organised from day one, then wedding planning will be a breeze.

To keep on top of any smaller lists you can use platforms such as Evernote, Asana, Trello, or any other productivity and team-based software.

Do you need to opt for a joint email address?

A bespoke email address has become quite common. It's easy to set up and means either you or your partner can create, access and respond to emails from one address without any confusion. In theory the idea is great, however I often find that couples still end up using their personal email addresses. Let's be honest, some of us love technology and others loathe it. For some, the very idea of setting up another inbox to respond to makes them feel anxious. If this is you, then I would personally avoid creating a separate email address and simply make your own wedding folder within an existing inbox that you use.

If one person is going to be taking the wedding planning lead, then, again, there really seems to be no need to create a separate email account as you can simply cc your partner in, or of course pop any useful contents inside a shared cloud, eliminating the need for them to read anything that isn't of much importance.

However, if you and your partner are both going to be heavily involved in the planning process and already have clogged inboxes at work, then having a separate wedding account isn't a bad idea. If you don't want wedding planning to take over your life, avoid setting up access to this email account on your phone or laptop so that your only choice is to access it via an internet browser – *at a time that is convenient for you*. This way you can dip in and out of wedding planning whenever you feel like. Having some space from the process is important and we will be diving into the mindset side of things further on in the book. Of course, if you love wedding planning like I do and feel like space isn't a necessity, that is absolutely fine too. The aim of this book is to help you enjoy the process, whichever approach you decide to take.

So far we've looked at what your immediate next steps should be after your engagement and made a note of the order in which you should most likely start ticking off suppliers. We will cover how you can find the best suppliers for your wedding in a later section of the book, but our next goal is to figure out exactly what your dream wedding looks like. Before we get stuck into the fun part, be sure to answer the questions at the end of this chapter.

Exercise:

1. Write down the top three things that matter most for your wedding.

(1)..

(2)..

(3)..

2. Where will you be storing all of your wedding documentation?

3. Will you be setting up a joint email address?

The Fun Begins

July 2017

Costa Coffee, Manchester

Selena sighed as she looked at her watch. He was fifteen minutes late. Again. The coffee shop was bustling with people looking to grab a quick lunch, which meant she couldn't even get up to order a drink out of fear that someone might take their chairs, or worse, *something else*. Scattered across the table was her MacBook, a notebook and pen, a stack of bridal and travel magazines and of course her favourite companion in life – *her phone*. She turned to her left and stared through the large window, thinking about having to leave all this behind. Moving to London had never really been on her radar – but then again, neither had marriage. That's when she saw him, leaping down the street with his phone held up to his ear and a grin plastered across his face. He walked right up to the window and blew her a kiss, mouthing *sorry* before heading towards the door. It was hard to stay mad at him for very long. That charming nature of his was sometimes so infuriating.

'Hun, I'm sorry. The train was late. There was nothing I could do! Hope you haven't been waiting too long.' He shrugged off his jacket, placing it on the back of a chair.

'At least you have the train to blame this time.'

'What will you have? Soy vanilla latte? Shall I get us a slice of cake to share?'

She nodded, with a half-smile.

As he waited in line, she opened up the spreadsheets on her laptop so they could do a quick recap, knowing full well he wouldn't have looked at a thing since their last conversation. She'd also started to bookmark her favourite wedding locations (*local and overseas*) all with one thing in common – plenty of open space for them to have an outdoor ceremony and no buildings in sight for miles to spoil the view. They'd finally managed to agree on a rough budget for the wedding, which would be split in half between the two families, though she was secretly worried it was going to start creeping up with the expensive ideas his parents had in mind. It wasn't so much the ideas she disliked, but the amount of money they were going to cost. She knew she had expensive taste herself, but she was also very aware that her family were not as financially secure as Rishi's, meaning compromises would need to be made.

'I spoke to my colleague at work – the one who got married in Santorini last year – and he said he'll ask his wife to email across details of all the suppliers they used.'

'Great…' she said, sliding the magazines to the windowsill to make room for the overflowing tray in his hand.

'I thought you'd be a little more excited, considering you've had your heart set on the place since we returned home after the engagement.'

He sat down and handed her a spoon for the cake.

'I do love the idea and I'm so grateful for the help, but… I've been looking at costings, practicalities and our guest list and it's working out to be a lot more than we thought.'

She turned her laptop towards him so he could see the budget breakdown on her screen.

'We can make these figures work,' he said reassuringly.

Numbers were his speciality and she knew he meant well, but her heart sank. Deep down she knew things wouldn't be so simple.

'Let's speak to the suppliers and then make a decision,' she said, pulling in the plate of cake towards her. Rishi knew it was his last chance to sneak in a bite before she demolished it all. After a few mouthfuls, she hovered her fingers over the trackpad, closed the budget spreadsheet and proudly opened up the dozen Pinterest boards she'd been working on. Rishi looked on as she went from deflated to animated in a split second when she started talking through the florals, outfits and food. He pretended to pay attention when in reality he was trying to comprehend how she had even found the time to put it all together between work, gym and family commitments. Though the boards were of little interest to him, seeing her so happy in that moment filled him with contentment.

Chapter Two

What Does Your Dream Wedding Look Like?

In the previous chapter, we explored the idea of following a structure when it comes to planning your wedding. By now you will have answered some of the bigger questions about your day and figured out what truly matters the most. You'll also have some sort of idea about how you'd like to store all the information that you will be collating over the next year or so. I'm being completely presumptuous in assuming there's a year to go, when in reality it could be a couple of months or two years. Whatever your time frame, it doesn't matter. The beauty of this book is that you can work through it with a timeline in mind that suits you. While the previous section focused on the practicalities, this chapter is about your vision.

I hope you're excited, because if you're anything like me you're just going to *love* this part. It's where we get to dream and be creative without thinking about logistics or money or practicalities. Have I got your attention? I sure hope so! Every wedding starts off with a vision. And by this, I mean: what kind of wedding do you really want? When I speak to my clients for the first time on a consultation call, I like to work through a set list of questions because learning about their vision is crucial for me. For example, I'll want to know what sort of backdrop they visualise for their ceremony, if they want a live band or a DJ, whether they want drinks and food to be free-flowing and informal or if they prefer things to be more structured and traditional. These things help me understand not just the amount of money they'll probably need to set aside, but also allow me learn more about their personalities, which determine the type of suppliers and items I will be recommending to them going forward.

Do you slide into the city chic category? Perhaps your vibe is more relaxed boho or rustic and eco-friendly? Don't worry – you don't need to fit neatly into any of the above categories. Truth be told, you might not even know what your own style is *yet* – things will become a lot clearer by the end of this section. One piece of advice that I strongly stand by is that you should try and avoid choosing things for your big day simply because they seem to be on trend. While there will always be things that are particularly popular each year, I personally don't believe there is such a thing as a "trendy" wedding. For me, each wedding should be personal to the couple and reflective of the type of people they are. If you stay true to your own personality, then your wedding details will flow naturally and come together without feeling forced.

I asked you in the previous chapter to make a top three list about what matters most. In this section, our goal is to narrow down your top three "dreamy desires". In case you're wondering, yes, I do have a slight fascination with the number three. (On a complete side note, I use Michael Hyatt's Full Focus Planner, which focuses on the power of the number three, on a daily basis to plan my time.) The theory behind this is simple: if we limit our list(s) to just three key things, then we are forced to select only the most important. These top three things will act as your anchor. I use this anchor to plan out my day. For you, this list will navigate the direction of your wedding planning.

Let's look at how your dreamy desires differ from what matters most. First of all, it's important to remember the what-matters-most list will trump every other list *every single time*. It's why we completed it first. These are the things that matter to you deeply that you simply can't imagine having a wedding without. Your desires, on the other hand, are things that you'd love to have. There are no rules here. You might want to make your entrance on a boat, get married in a palace, or have your ceremony at sunset. These things will tend to be more visual or materialistic aspects of the day, rather than things that drive you emotionally. Your desires will make you feel excited and alive, because quite often they might feel a little out of reach. But being out of reach isn't necessarily a bad thing!

This list will help you understand what your heart truly desires, allowing you to centre other aspects of your day around this. For instance, if you want to make your entrance on a boat, even if this doesn't seem possible, you'll discover that being near water is important to you and can keep this on your agenda when you start looking for a venue.

It's also important to bear in mind that sometimes what you think you want on a material level (desire) doesn't necessarily match what you want on an emotional level. If you figure this out at the start, it will help you clearly navigate the direction of your wedding going forward, rather than lead you down a confusing path that ends with you trying to find two very different things from a very confused supplier. For example, our bride, Selena, had her heart set on getting married in Greece because it played a special part in her relationship with Rishi. However, we know she has financial concerns about that location, and what's more, one of her non-negotiables (which you won't be aware of) is that every member of her immediate family is in attendance at the wedding, including her grandparents. This shows us that she likes scenic, meaningful locations and of course has her heart set on an outdoor wedding.

I've had clients who on many occasions have decided against having their wedding at independent manor houses (desire) purely based on the fact that it didn't provide the flexibility and comfort they required for their guests (what matters most). Other clients have happily moved forward with a venue in the middle of nowhere and halved their guest list to make it happen, because a beautiful setting was on both their "what matters most" and "dreamy desires" lists. There's no right or wrong with either, as long as you follow your heart.

Once you've made your top three "dreamy desires" list, it's time for you to start working on some visual inspiration. Before I continue, let me reiterate that this task is supposed to be lots of fun! Get yourself in the zone; put on some upbeat music, make yourself a coffee, grab yourself a slice of cake – do whatever you need to find your inner J. Lo (you know, from *The Wedding Planner*!). Your task is to create some mood boards of your ideal day. You can do this using Pinterest alone, or look towards Instagram or wedding supplier websites for some extra inspiration. Your initial images will probably stem from your desires list, but you'll soon find plenty of things you fall in love with along the way. The more images you collect, the clearer your style will become (provided that they follow a similar theme).

You can create separate boards for different colour palettes or specific items such as florals, cakes, outfits, hair and make-up looks, etc. It's basically your board so you're in charge. If both you and your partner are heavily involved in the planning process together then it is definitely worth you doing this exercise separately at first, and then finding a middle ground (as suggested in Chapter One). Although trying to get any groom to create a Pinterest board is probably going to prove a task in itself, so good luck! If it's the first time you're using Pinterest it can be a little tricky to get your head around, but there are plenty of blog posts and YouTube videos that will explain what you need to do. One thing I would certainly encourage is that you keep your boards private, particularly if you plan on surprising your guests on the day.

If you're taking the lead when it comes to aesthetics and overall planning, then your next goal will be to communicate this vision to your partner, family and suppliers. Communicating ideas is so much easier when you have something visual to showcase, which is why creating those boards is crucial.

Exercise:

1. Write down your top three dreamy desires.

(1) ....

(2) ....

(3) ....

2. Start putting together at least one mood board that represents your wedding day.

3. Do you see a particular theme developing with your mood board? If so, what does this tell you about your style?

The Zoom Calendar

August 2017
A casual Thursday evening at home

Selena sank into the sofa with a freshly blended protein smoothie in her hand. She'd had a strenuous day at work debating Instagram strategies for her new fashion client, and quite frankly wanted nothing more than to kick back and watch the next episode of *Four More Shots Please!* on Amazon Prime. But sadly, wedding planning duty called. She leaned forward towards the coffee table and flipped open her MacBook, placing her smoothie on a coaster nearby.

'Hey gorgeous, how was work?' said the beaming face on the other side of the screen.

'Pretty draining, but they treated us to a three-course lunch, which definitely did not help my wedding diet,' she joked.

Rishi could see how tired she looked and knew full well that she'd be knocked out the moment her head hit the pillow. They'd been catching up every Tuesday and Thursday evening for the past three weeks for their virtual wedding planning meets, leaving the weekends free to catch up with their parents and scout for venues. Long-distance planning was tough, and he could already feel it taking its toll.

'So, I spoke to my parents about the guest list and we think we can get it down to one hundred from our end.'

'Wow! Are you serious?' she exclaimed, feeling both shocked and a little envious. 'Listen, there's no way my mum and dad are going to get it down to below two hundred. I know this means the castle is out of the question, but I just don't know what to do.'

The guest list was becoming a real issue in Selena's household and they'd only just managed to reduce the number down to two hundred after many, many arguments. And the fallout with non-invited family members was yet to come. It's not that she didn't appreciate where her parents were coming from – she was an only child with a large extended family and this was her parents' one chance to get everything right – but she was fed up of having to make compromises. The idea of a destination wedding was already out the window due to practicalities and finding a location halfway between Manchester and London that ticked *every one* of their requirements was proving to be impossible. Someone was going to have to give up something and this time it wasn't going to be her. How could she be this fed up before the planning process had even really begun?

'Well, is it worth maybe crunching the figures again to see if we can afford to have the bigger manor house? It's kind of perfect and an exclusive hire.'

'Sure, let's have a chat with the parents over the weekend and see,' she said, knowing full well that even their absolute maximum budget was already stretched.

'And then we'll catch up at yours with my parents the following week to run through what we have so far.'

'Yes. I think the mums need to go over the wedding ceremony before we even start looking for a priest.'

'Anything else?'

'Do you think we need some help…?'

'What kind?'

'Wedding planning help! I've been speaking to some friends who said that most people hire a wedding planner nowadays and I'm starting to see why. Maybe I should have a look at a few.'

'If it means less work for me then I'd definitely be up for that.' He smiled.

She rolled her eyes and took a sip of the smoothie. 'Well, that was easy. Let's call it a night and I'll text you tomorrow. Love you.'

'Night. Love you too.'

She pushed the screen to a close, swung her legs to the side and curled up on the sofa, wrapping her hands around a pillow. There was so much to do and she really had no idea how she was going to get it all done.

Rishi switched off his desktop and took a deep breath as he ran his fingers through his hair. He could see that finances were becoming a problem, particularly as his parents saw the wedding as a social event rather than the intimate family affair he and Selena had imagined. He didn't want to offer to contribute more money in case it came across as insensitive to her family, but he also knew his parents would not be happy to make cutbacks in certain areas. He felt like he was being pulled in two different directions and was starting to disappoint everyone around him.

Chapter Three

How Do You Communicate Your Vision?

So by this point you will have made your beautiful boards and will have a much clearer idea of the type of wedding that you'd like. You're now ready to reach for your practical wedding planning hat. We need to think about how we're going to make your ideas and dreams a reality. The aesthetics of weddings have changed massively since the emergence of platforms like Pinterest and Instagram. While they are both a godsend and every bride's best friend during the planning process (aside from her wedding planner, of course), they can also act as a slight hindrance. Let me explain: it's important to use your boards for inspiration, or as a starting point, rather than view them as your desired end result. This isn't to say that you cannot recreate some of the stunning visuals that you have probably pinned, but you'll be setting yourself up for a pretty big disappointment if you are expecting your day to look like an exact replica. A lot of what you eventually choose will come down to your overall budget (along with other logistical practicalities).

As we discovered in the previous chapter, your desires may not always come to life (and this is okay), but they will certainly help you make clearer decisions along the way. How many of us have dreamed of jetting off to a private island in first class? Now imagine this: even if first-class travel isn't feasible for you, you could actually put together your own little travel pamper pack filled with luxury mini toiletries and get your favourite meal wrapped up as a takeout from the airport to eat on the flight. If you don't quite make it to a private island you could still upgrade to having your own private luxury villa. Not getting your original *desire* does not mean you won't have the best holiday of your life – it just means you have to get a little creative to ensure your money goes a long way, and it's exactly the same when it comes to planning your wedding.

So how should you use your board if you aren't looking to replicate it for your big day?

If you've pinned lots of light, airy images with soft colours on your mood boards, then when it comes to choosing your photographer these are the sort of shots you should be looking out for in their portfolios – stay away from dark and moody styles. Or let's say you want to start looking for your outfit – it may make more sense for you to stay away from traditional reds and maroons and look at pastel shades instead. These are real examples of how to use your boards effectively to help navigate the wedding planning process. Now would be a great time for you to break down your mood boards and figure out how to make them a reality, or how to use these ideas to help navigate the planning process. Once you fully understand what you actually want, it's time to communicate this with everyone else – starting with your partner.

If you don't share the same vision as your partner, the next best thing is to find a middle ground. You both need to be clear about what you want as a couple before you approach any suppliers or discuss the day with anyone else. A united front is the key to successful wedding planning. If you find that you and your partner have completely different taste, which is a very real possibility, then try and split up the tasks between you. For example, it's quite common for brides to become very involved with the florals and centrepieces for a wedding reception, while the groom's main concern is the sound and lighting. If this is the case for you, then it makes perfect sense for each of you to take charge of your respective areas and feel satisfied with the end result, rather than feel like you're having to battle and compromise your way through the whole process.

You need to think about splitting the responsibility of the wedding elements rather than compromising on every tiny wedding detail, because if you don't, you'll feel the frustration bubbling up inside you ready to explode at any moment. Think of wedding planning like driving to a nominated destination. Imagine you're in the driving seat and your partner is in the passenger seat. You're determined to follow Google Maps whereas your partner is old school and prefers to follow a physical map. (Seriously, who looks at those nowadays?) Anyway, if you start to follow Google Maps but then switch at the next turn to follow your physical map, you may end up going round in circles because both maps are following completely different routes, even though they both lead to the same place.

Now, let's explore this analogy within a wedding. You and your partner obviously have the same goal in mind, which is to have the best wedding ever! But, your idea on making it the best wedding or how to get there may be slightly different. Unless you both get on the same page (or map) you're going to end up going round in circles and getting very irritated with each other. Plus, with no clear style or theme, things are definitely not going to look pretty on the day.

What should you do if you and your partner can't find a middle ground? I'm not going to lie, there may be times when neither you nor your partner can seem to find a compromise. If this happens, don't feel like your world is going to come crashing down, because I promise it's not. Below I'm going to share some insider advice on how you can keep the peace. Don't be tempted to skip straight to that section. First, let's have a look at some of the common topics that are likely to cause a minor (or major) dispute and how you can find a middle ground.

Number of guests

The number of guests is always going to be tricky when it comes to planning an Indian or interfaith wedding. More often than not, the pressure to increase the guest list will come from your families and it is always good to have some sort of answer in place for when your families start asking you to add extra people to the list. But let's not stereotype completely – there are instances where couples themselves have a large guest list and find it difficult to narrow things down. Either way, you're going to need to find a compromise.

What to do: You and your partner need to have a clear guest-list policy in place that applies to both families. Try and split your numbers fifty-fifty if you can so things remain equal and fair. If one of you has a larger family than the other, then do take this into consideration. Make two lists if need be. One with guests whom you cannot have the wedding without and another list filled with guests whom you'd love to invite but are not necessarily *essential*.

Food

It's strange to imagine arguments taking place over food choices, but it has been known to happen. Problems often arise when you have two different sets of guests who will be looking for different things from your menu. One of you may have predominantly vegan or vegetarian guests, while the other may be inviting avid meat eaters. Or you might have guests from two completely different cultural backgrounds with different palates.

What to do: For the first dilemma, if you really can't find a compromise then it's worth trying to seat any strict vegan and vegetarian guests together and avoid any meat dishes being served to their table. If you've got guests with completely different tastes, then I would suggest opting for a fusion menu. That way everybody wins.

Alcohol

Should you opt for an open bar, provide your own alcohol, or hire an external company? Do you need to have wine on the tables or have some champagne floating around for any toasts? There are lots of questions and differences of opinion around the subject of alcohol, which makes things tricky. More often than not, any disagreements here will arise due to the costs involved.

What to do: The short and simple answer is to go with whatever you feel comfortable with as there are no strict rules – provided you aren't marrying someone whose culture prohibits the consumption of alcohol. Most guests will expect a selection of alcoholic and non-alcoholic beverages to be served on a complimentary basis, so as long as you have something, you're pretty good to go. If the budget is tight, make a list of the type of drinks your guests are most likely to consume and have a limited bar. Your bar spend can be anything from £2,000 to £20,000 plus alone. If you're really stuck, hold off until you get to the budget section and then determine what you can afford to do.

Wedding ceremony

Your legal ceremony will be fairly straightforward, however it's amazing how many different variations there can be of the same religious ceremony. A lot of these variations will depend on how involved and religious your respective families are.

What to do: Have a conversation with both families present to discuss how you'd like the ceremony conducted. You'll need to go through this step by step to iron out all of the details. If you can't come to an agreement, it's definitely worth getting a priest involved to act as a mediator and to also advise what would work best.

While these are some of the most common areas that cause disputes, they are certainly not limited to these topics. Nevertheless, in most cases you will find that it's fairly easy to come to a compromise. But, just in case you're struggling to get there, I did promise to share an insider tip with you, so here goes...

If you just can't seem to find a happy balance, then I would suggest both you and your partner take charge of different events regardless of whether or not you're splitting the bill in half. This means that while you both have input in both events, one person has a clear veto power to make a firm decision. It's not an approach I would explore without trying to find a compromise and it may feel a little controversial, but it's definitely a good way to keep the peace!

So by this stage we're clear that you and your partner need to be on the same page and hopefully you have some clarity on how you get there. The second stage is to get the parents involved. You and your partner need to know what you want as a couple before you start going backwards and forwards with suggestions from your parents (or anyone else, including your suppliers) because they *will* make suggestions, and it can cause an upset. Let's take the example of Rishi and Selena. We've started to learn that both of their families are quite different and have different ideas about their wedding. The main thing is that, despite any differences, Rishi and Selena have kept a united front while being respectful of each other's needs. They're trying to find a compromise and a solution that works for everyone.

It's extremely important to maintain a sense of calm, as no one wants to start off married life on a sour note, particularly with their in-laws. And though I don't love using this analogy when it comes to wedding planning (because the process is certainly not a "battle" and should never feel like one), it's true what they say: you really do need to pick your battles. You aren't going to win every round. If you intend to keep the peace then you may have to let a few things slide. You will find a whole load of books on the art of negotiation and if you really do find yourself being backed into a corner by someone then these would certainly be worth a read. From personal experience, I have often found if you let someone think they've got the upper hand (even if they haven't) they're usually pretty happy.

This doesn't apply to every case, but sometimes the reason things turn sour is because someone feels let down or, in all honesty, a little unloved. Let's face it, everyone gets excited over a wedding, but they can soon start to feel pretty deflated when they realise you don't really want them involved in the planning process at all. If anyone is behaving a little out of turn or having a bit of sulk, it's probably because they're disappointed that you don't need their help. After all, everyone likes to feel needed. So, if you find yourself in a situation where people are trying to get involved in certain aspects of planning that you'd rather they leave to you, then think about how you can keep them busy. It's certainly worth giving this a try if it could ease any tensions, don't you think?

Now if you're wondering how to keep someone busy, then my best advice is to give them sole responsibility for their own mini project. For example, ask your mum to be in charge of organising your wedding ceremony items. Request your best friend to arrange the wedding garlands. Your mother-in-law might be delighted at the thought of helping you finalise the canapés. Delegating tasks doesn't just help you out, it helps those closest to you feel valued. It's a win-win!

Trust me when I say you're going to need as much love and support from your family and friends as you can get. Do not push them aside, and be sure to keep your emotions in check, which leads us on to the next chapter.

Exercise:

1. Have a chat with your partner to determine if there are any ideas that you don't agree on. If so, make a list of these and how you intend on finding a middle ground.

2. Make a list of any tasks that you could potentially delegate to friends or family members.

3. Run through your vision for your wedding ceremony with your partner and both sets of parents – this is a must! Do you have the same idea or is this something you need to work through together?

The Clash Of The Parents

August 2017
Lunch at the Chauhans' in Manchester

'Mum, stop fussing over the samosas. The Mehtas will be here any minute!' Selena screamed down from her bedroom. Her mum was overworked, overstressed and overthinking *everything*. Together with her gran, they had cooked up a feast large enough to feed the entire street. And if that wasn't enough, they had roped her in to help, when instead, Selena should have been going through her wedding spreadsheets again. The Mehtas would be more impressed with a professional Excel doc than a homemade samosa. In fact, her mother-in-law probably wouldn't even be able to comprehend why anyone would wake up at 6am to start folding pastry when they could simply pop in to a shop and buy it.

The two families were such polar opposites, with the two mums living in completely different worlds. Her mum could tell you the best herbal remedy to get rid of a cold or cook up a batch of freshly fried pakoras in an instant, whereas Rishi's mum could state the exact price of a wine bottle from a single sip or get you a table at any booked-out restaurant in London. Come to think of it, Selena definitely had the best of both worlds, but when those two worlds collided, things seemed to feel a little…clunky.

She sped down the stairs as she heard the car approach and waited for the bell to ring before she opened the door. She counted to three (because that felt like an appropriate amount of time to wait), took in a deep breath and turned the knob.

'Uncle, Aunty, come in.'

'And I'll just stand outside, shall I?' Rishi teased.

'Stop being a pain and come in.' She smirked.

The parents smiled, hugged, did their namastes and went straight into the dining room.

'Selena, beta, will you bring your gran and grandad through?' her mum called.

The eight of them huddled over the six-seater table, which felt like a tight squeeze given all the items her mum had laid out. It felt strange sitting together, as it was customary for men to be served first in their household. However, Rishi's dad insisted that everyone should sit down straight away so there was enough time to run through the wedding details and make it back to London before dark.

'How is everything coming along?' asked Mr Mehta, looking straight towards Rishi and Selena. Selena looked down.

'Good…we think. We just need to figure out the final guest numbers before we book the venue,' said Rishi.

'Oh, and we're thinking about hiring a wedding planner,' added Selena.

'What?' Her mother seemed perplexed. 'What do you need a planner for if you are doing all the planning?'

'Mum, the planner helps to make sure everything is perfect so that no one else is stressed on the wedding day.'

'Honestly, in our day there were no such things as planners. Your parents chose everything, and the bride and groom just turned up. And, beta, *you will be stressed*. Every bride is stressed. It's normal.'

'That wasn't the case at our wedding,' said Mrs Mehta.

Selena glared at her mum to stop her responding in an inappropriate manner. She couldn't wait for lunch to be over so they could have a level-headed conversation. But things only went from bad to worse. It was clear Rishi's parents were not going to back down on the venue choice. They had well-known dignitaries on their guest list and Rishi was their eldest son – and the *first* to get married. Selena's parents made it clear that paying £30,000 for a venue was extortionate and something they didn't feel comfortable with. To make matters worse, the Mehtas wanted a silent wedding ceremony conducted in English, while the Chauhans wanted a traditional ceremony without unnecessary *modern* interference. It was all in all a full-blown disaster that had left Selena and Rishi with more questions than answers and an eight-page Word doc filled with notes.

As they walked out the door, Rishi turned round and looked at her. 'I'll call you later.'

She nodded in agreement, feeling rather deflated.

'Don't worry, we'll work it out,' he whispered, as he gave her a goodbye kiss on the cheek.

'Sure,' she lied.

Chapter Four

How To Successfully Manage Your Emotions

As a bride there are so many emotions you're going to be tackling at the same time, with fear being right at the top of that list. You might fear getting ripped off by your suppliers or worse – your suppliers not actually doing what they're told. Combine this with the fear of disappointing your partner, parents and guests and you're suddenly at risk of disappearing down a dark black hole in which you won't enjoy this process at all. This is *not* what we want.

Let's take Selena as an example. On top of her financial concerns and wedding planning dramas, she's trying to come to terms with the fact that she's going to have to say goodbye to the place she's called home for twenty-nine years. Of course she loves Rishi, but the thought of leaving behind her family and friends, job, gym and even her local coffee shop feels pretty overwhelming. There's a different level of fear that comes with having to start your life from scratch in a big new city.

Whether you're dealing with something similar or something entirely different, I want you to know that the feelings you're experiencing at the moment are completely normal. In all honesty, they're some of the key reasons why so many brides come to me looking for one-to-one help. A lot of these brides have so much going on in their day-to-day lives that they simply don't have the energy to deal with an extra layer of stress and pressure.

This is why I developed my *Planned To Perfection* wedding planning community. Within it, I've created a clear step-by-step system for brides to follow, with the added bonus of direct access to me – meaning they can simply fire across a question knowing full well that someone has their back. I understand the importance of having someone to guide and talk you through your wedding planning journey as I believe that sometimes even a little bit of reassurance can go a really long way. What's more, these brides receive support and advice from others who are in the same boat – this is what makes it so special. So I would advise you to find your own support system – because having people by your side makes all the difference.

One thing I need you to make note of and underline right now is that no matter what obstacle you're facing, you *will* overcome it. Just go back a second and think about all the difficult challenges you've had to face in life. Can you remember the very first time you got behind the wheel of a car or travelled on your own? Maybe your biggest challenge was moving away from home, passing your final exams or getting over a break-up. We all face incredibly tough challenges on a daily basis, and I'm pretty confident that you probably came out on top with everything you've faced before – your wedding will be no different. Don't focus on all the uncertainties; focus on your own strengths. You've totally got this!

I say this with full confidence because I understand your fear. I felt sick to my stomach when I went on-site to manage my first-ever event. I was nervous, scared and excited all rolled into one. I'd been planning the event with my client for over a year and wanted their wedding day to be absolutely perfect! I didn't actually have a whole lot of experience behind me at the time, but I did have plenty of passion, drive and enthusiasm, which basically carried me through. Had I let doubts creep in from the back of my mind that I wasn't good enough, or I didn't know what I was doing, or that I was going to screw it all up, then there's a very good chance that I would have crumbled on the day. So, I fully understand how you feel, and trust me, there's absolutely no way that I'm going to let you fall short! I want you to stand tall with confidence after reading this chapter, because together we are going to ensure that your day is nothing short of brilliant.

I'm actually writing this book during the Covid-19 lockdown (a period I'm sure many of us will remember vividly over the coming years) and as you can imagine, this has been perhaps one of the most testing times for couples and wedding suppliers. In a bid to get couples through this difficult time, I launched a free wedding coaching group to help brides and grooms with their wedding challenges. One of the first things we talked about in this group was the power of a positive mindset. Below are a few suggestions for how you can maintain control of the planning process so that you can enjoy it.

1. Do some mindset work daily

Whether you prefer to read, meditate or journal – pick something and do it daily, even if it's just for five minutes. I'd recommend giving each of these things a try to see what really works for you. You can even try a combination! When we have mental clarity, we can see things from a different point of view and often understand them a little better.

2. Exercise

This probably sounds like a cliché, but if this isn't something you do regularly then it's definitely worth incorporating some sort of daily (or at least weekly) exercise into your routine. It can be as simple as a walk or a run, something more fun like a cardio class, or even some yoga. The release of serotonin in your body will instantly lift your mood and help you feel energised. Added bonus: you'll be in the best shape of your life for your big day.

3. Do what you love

I refuse to believe that only *some* people are creative. Everyone is creative in their own way. So find something you love and make some time to do it. Whether it's baking, knitting or writing – even if it's just once a month. Seriously, take some time out and focus on doing something you love because it's so good for the mind. If you simply can't think of anything at all, then I give you full permission to take a day off and binge-watch the latest series on Netflix. You can thank me later.

4. Stay in the zone

Always focus on what you can do and what you have control over at any given time rather than obsess over all the things that can't be done. Stressing over things you can't control isn't going to help anyone.

5. Stay organised

We touched on organisational methods in Chapter One. It's certainly worth revisiting if you need a quick refresher, but one of the best ways to remain calm is to keep on top of all of your documentation and communication. It's easy to start tying yourself up in knots if you lose track of what's going on – do not let this be you.

6. Take time out

I know you're excited about planning your wedding. You totally should be and it's probably one of the reasons why you bought this book! But, it is necessary to take some time out. By this I mean don't spend every free minute of your day planning your wedding. Schedule in a date night with your partner and make sure wedding talk is occasionally banned. Never lose sight of why you're putting in all this hard work in the first place. Your relationship always comes first.

7. Get external help

This is right at the bottom of the list because you may prefer to manage on your own, which is totally fine. However, if you're someone who struggles with the demands of a busy workload and hectic social life, and would really rather sit back and relax while someone else does all the heavy lifting, then hiring a wedding planner or coordinator is always an option. If you're a budget-conscious couple, then I would certainly recommend looking into booking in a seat at *Planned To Perfection* – where I've basically done all the hard work for you.

Essentially, you are going to be feeling A LOT of mixed emotions and the best way to deal with them is by controlling what you can. Most of the things mentioned above probably won't even cost you a penny (aside from hiring a planner). So, aren't they worth giving a go? Get started right away and you'll notice a difference within a week, if not less. Self-care is a must when you're dealing with stressful situations because if you cannot take care of yourself, then you will struggle to look out for everyone and everything around you. But what's more, wedding planning is such a special moment in your life, one that you won't get to experience again (and I truly hope you won't need to), so I want you to really enjoy it to the absolute max!

Now that you're ready to take on the world, are you ready to fully immerse yourself in the details of the planning process?

Exercise:

1. Decide what your support system will be. Who is going to help keep you in check and manage your emotions?

2. Make a list of your "wedding fears" then look at each fear closely and find a solution to prevent this fear from becoming a reality.

3. Outline how you're going to utilise your "me time" and work on your mindset and well-being.

Part Two

The Planning Process

In the previous section we focused on how to stay on top of your mindset and really tune in to what kind of wedding you want. This next part of the book is split into four essential chapters, which I believe are the key to mastering the wedding planning process.

Over the years, I've learned some really useful techniques that have enabled me to successfully plan and manage multiple events for my clients, which in turn has led to the growth of my business. I'll be sharing some key techniques I personally use which you can implement too in a bid to make the planning process a whole lot easier. I imagine that is one of the key reasons why you picked up this book. Together, we're going to focus on establishing a hassle-free, simple way to get things done!

By the end of this section you will have mapped out how to squeeze wedding planning time into your already hectic life and will also be clearer on your overall wedding budget and how much money you intend to spend on your key suppliers. A big part of this section is focused on distractions, or rather how to stop getting distracted – because in my experience this can often become the biggest downfall for many couples as they end up going off on a different tangent. And finally, we'll wrap up with my guide on how to find the best quality suppliers.

Turn the page to get started…

The Meltdown

August 2017
Unexpected mid-week catch up on the train

As the train started to pick up speed, Rishi felt a sigh of relief wash over him. It looked like he had the entire table to himself – and boy did he welcome the space. He loosened his tie and leaned back to rest his head. There's nothing quite like a four-hour meeting on a hot summer's day to tire you out. While he always loved meeting his pharmacy colleagues, he had been feeling somewhat mentally drained over the past few days. In between work, Selena, and keeping up with his parents, he was starting to feel stressed – a feeling that was quite alien to him. Decisions needed to be made and things weren't getting any easier. Rewind back to a year ago when he and Selena had just started dating – life seemed so carefree and easy. If this is what married life was going to always be like, he wasn't so sure it was for him.

Just as he closed his eyes, he heard his phone buzz. He pulled it out of his pocket and saw Selena's name flashing on the screen. It was odd for her to call in the middle of the working day. He instantly pressed on the touch screen and immediately pulled the phone to his ear.

'Hey, babe. What's up?'

'She won't…stand…I…planner!' she sobbed hysterically.

'Stop. Breathe. Come again?'

'My mum. She won't let me hire the planner. My parents have put their foot down. We had a huge argument and they just don't get it. I'm fed up. I don't think I want this anymore. Let's just elope!'

Usually Rishi would laugh off the comment with a joke, but he could hear how upset and frustrated she was.

'Nothing's working. The venue is over budget. The priest your mum wants charges two thousand pounds! Why do we need a band? Why can't we just have background music? And don't even get me started on the alcohol. My dad is going mental. But the worst part is, this wedding is everything we didn't want, Rish. It's about them and not about us. I don't want this.'

He turned down the volume from the side bar, feeling conscious the passengers nearby would hear her.

'I know it's all crazy. We need to sort this out, just you and me. We'll find a way to make both sets of parents happy, but first we need to figure out what we want.'

Rishi had a long journey home but stayed on the phone with her throughout to calm her nerves and stop her feeling so distraught. It was completely out of character for her to feel so beaten down, and so for the first time in a very long time they had an honest conversation and *really* listened to each other. They decided they wanted to have a plan in place before ending the call and this is exactly what they worked on.

They decided to go ahead with the manor house which they both loved and would keep his parents happy. They felt the couple of thousand pounds they'd set aside for the planner could go towards the extra cost and hopefully keep her parents happy. It wasn't a decision Selena was happy with, but she knew there was no extra pot of cash. She would rope in her bestie, Tash, who handled corporate events at work to oversee the paperwork and help with the planning. They also opted to tone down the florals (there are only so many fresh flowers a bride needs), swapped their band for a DJ, and finalised which caterer they wanted to move forward with. While it seemed to take them reaching rock bottom to climb back up, they'd made every pending decision in less than an hour by simply doing what they hadn't been doing all along – focusing on what mattered most. They looked back at their initial wedding vision – how they wanted to feel, what was most important to them and what was non-negotiable – and the moment they did this, everything seemed so much clearer. The only thing left was to tell the parents!

Chapter Five

How To Manage Your Time

My shelf at home is filled with self-help books focused on time management and productivity. As a solopreneur and wedding planner, I am busy working with multiple clients and multiple projects every single day, which means I am constantly looking for effective ways to get more done. Over the years, I've learned that one of the secrets to being productive is to find a way to work smarter, not necessarily harder – and I want you to focus on the same.

There's no doubt in my mind that you are probably juggling multiple things, so much so that finding some spare time to read this book alone might have been a struggle. If this is how you currently feel, I get it. I've had many days, months and weeks where it's been a struggle to get even the simplest of things done, but at some stage in my self-help reading journey I discovered that it's up to *you* to make time for the things that are important in your life. You have to hold yourself accountable and make your goals non-negotiable. For example, I love to read, but I was struggling to find the time to read a physical book and kept pushing it on the back burner. Then I got to thinking…how do I keep myself accountable? Now, this might sound a little out there, but I actually went on to launch a virtual book club *just* to ensure that I read a minimum of twelve books per year without making any excuses. I wanted to be accountable to someone else (or in my case seventy other people, and counting). And guess what? It's working. You can use a similar approach for anything you want to get done – including *planning your wedding*.

Some of you reading this book will be fine and may find that you have more than enough time to plan your wedding. Your struggle lies somewhere else, and if that's the case, then other parts of the book will certainly resonate with you more closely. However, if, like me, you excel when you're held accountable, then I would highly encourage you to find something, or someone, to help you stay on track. As an example, at the end of my live weekly wedding Q&As for *Planned To Perfection*, I always ask my brides what they'll be working on for the next seven days. That way, when I see them the following week I can check in and see if it actually got done. If not, we can discuss why and find a way around the obstacles.

So how long does it take to plan a wedding? Well, pinpointing an actual number is going to be difficult, as each couple will have a different set of requirements or a different number of events as part of their wedding celebrations. According to one study, it can take up to 528* hours to plan a wedding! Before your head starts spinning into a frenzy, just take a moment to breathe. This is obviously *a lot* of time, possibly even double what you were thinking, but I promise it is totally manageable if you break it down.

528 hours ÷ 18 (because a lot of couples tend to start planning around a year and a half before the big day) = 29.3 hours a month

29.3 hours ÷ 4 = 7.3 hours a week

7.3 hours ÷ 7 = 1 hour a day

Now one hour a day seems much more manageable and realistic, don't you think? I'm not saying that you should be expecting to spend one hour every day for the next eighteen months planning your wedding, but this approximate measure will allow you to start scheduling in some time. You could spread this out over three days or combine it into one day over the weekend. You may have some free time where you can speed up the process and get two weeks' worth of work done and then not plan for a couple of weeks. How you manage your time is entirely up to you, as long as you find some way to manage it.

If you can find time to binge-watch a box set on Netflix, go out to a restaurant or watch a Bollywood film, then trust me, you have enough time to plan your wedding. Sometimes it can feel daunting to find even a few hours a week – I get it. So, let's have a look at some techniques that you can use:

People generally fall into two different categories: those who like to time-block and those who like to work in smaller bite-size chunks. The former will prefer to block out perhaps half a day or a full day to focus on one task, whereas the latter will prefer to work in shorter bursts. For example, you might prefer waking up thirty minutes earlier every day to get tasks completed. Personally, I tend to work best when I block out a significant chunk of time to get something done so my brain is only focusing on one thing for a larger part of the day. Studies show that when we're switching from one task to another, we actually end up not working to our full capacity.

By no means do I want to put you off planning a wedding by referring to it as *work*, but if you treat it as a "work" project that you schedule in your calendar, you're going to be more likely to stick to it and get things done, resulting in less stress and anxiety.

> **Top tip:** Once you've blocked out your wedding planning time in your calendar, make it non-negotiable. This means if an invite comes along for some after-work drinks, or a friend invites you out for dinner, say you're busy and reschedule for a time you do have available in your calendar.

We'll be covering distractions in a later chapter, however it's clear that these should be kept to a minimum when you're trying to get through your tasks. Additional techniques to help make things easier are:

1. Plan in advance

Decide what you need to get done in advance, and once it's done, step away (unless you really feel inclined to do more). This way you have a specific goal with a deadline. If you try and do everything all at once you're going to drive yourself crazy.

2. Don't check your email all the time

Do you ever feel the need to reply to messages or emails the moment they land in your inbox? If this is you, then you need to revisit the very first chapter and create a separate inbox to plan your wedding. As a supplier I understand the need to reply to people in a timely manner more than most – so set aside a specific day (or few days) in the week where you'll log in and answer any messages. This will free up time to get other non-wedding-related things done in the week and you'll feel in control of the planning process rather than feeling like it's controlling you.

3. Find your flow

As mentioned earlier, you might prefer to work in smaller chunks or block out a larger time frame. Maybe you prefer working on your wedding at night or in the morning, during the weekdays or the weekend, over a coffee at your local café, or from the comfort of your living room. Find what works for you and stick to it – you can even offer yourself a little treat as you work through certain milestones.

4. Eat the frog

This means prioritising your tasks and getting the most important things done first, no matter how boring. For instance, looking for cake makers and booking in food tastings may seem like much more fun than logging in budgets on a finance spreadsheet, but if you keep putting the spreadsheet off it will keep wearing you down. Instead, if you get it out of the way then you won't feel guilty for carrying on with the "fun stuff".

5. Stop multitasking

This means stop trying to find all of your suppliers and do everything all at once. You can't look for your venue, find your make-up artist and finalise your florist all at the same time. Set out your structure and order and stick to it. Sometimes you'll need to deviate a little depending on supplier response times or your own priorities, but remember it's okay to take your time. Your wedding day is important, and you want to ensure that you get everything right.

These are a few tips to get you started but I would also highly recommend that you complete the exercise below:

Exercise:

1. Look at your calendar and block out your wedding planning time for the next week, month or three months (whatever time frame you feel most comfortable with).

2. Make a list of what you will complete during each of these wedding time blocks.

3. Set clear deadlines for when each individual task needs to be completed by.

˙source
https://www.independent.co.uk/life-style/dating/wedding-planning-time-venue-dress-food-price-engagement-a8788076.html
Study conducted by Minted https://www.minted.com

The Numbers Game

September 2017
Weekly wedding catch-up call

'Our finances are solid. Don't worry, everything's right on track,' Rishi lied. Though their finances weren't out of control, the spreadsheet in front of him was telling him that it would be highly unlikely they'd get everything they wanted within budget. How could they when so many people were involved? Even though his parents had calmed down, and he and Selena had made most of the major decisions, he still felt like he was being pulled in two different directions. Though he wanted his fiancée to be as happy as could be, he was also mindful of the fact that his parents had probably been dreaming about his wedding day before he was even born. Though it often seemed like they were more concerned about keeping up appearances, he knew deep down they really just wanted the best for their eldest son – and perhaps the only son of theirs to get married.

Rishi's younger brother Rahul lived in New York and only came to the UK once a year at Christmas or to meet up with the three of them for their annual family vacation. Even if Rahul did surprisingly end up tying the knot, they all knew the guest list would be incredibly small and most likely limited to a dozen or so family members at best – hence the extra pressure Rishi felt to please his parents.

He knew the Chauhans were already exceeding their budget and certainly didn't want to put any additional strain on them. He also didn't want to go behind Selena's back and make secret payments from his own account without telling her. It was important to start their new life together with respect and complete honesty. So after a lot of deliberation, he decided there was only one thing left to do – even if it did cause a bit of tension. He would simply speak to Selena and her parents and explain that while he and his parents appreciated their budget restrictions, they also had certain elements they wanted to include at the wedding – elements that they would happily pay for separately. It wasn't ideal, but it was the most practical approach to ensure everyone got what they wanted.

'So how much do we have left to spend on the cake?' Selena asked. Her excited voice rang in his ears a little too loudly through his AirPods.

'Really, the cake is your biggest concern?'

'Of course! I haven't had a decent dessert in months thanks to this wedding diet, so our wedding cake needs to be amazing. I intend on grabbing the biggest slice and savouring every single mouthful!'

'You're insane, you know that?' he teased. He knew how much she loved her cake and as a surprise had actually lined up a meeting with a celebrity baker, who just happened to be dating a friend of his. The baker had promised to design and deliver a wedding cake of their choice for free, in return for them agreeing to be part of her web series. The only catch: the cake had to be extravagant as no one wanted to watch a boring cake being made on screen. In his head it was a no-brainer, but he had to get the official sign-off from Selena, though he couldn't imagine her refusing a showstopper cake – especially one she didn't have to pay for.

If only they'd managed to score a few more deals. It certainly would have struck off an extra zero from the number at the bottom of his budget spreadsheet.

Chapter Six

How To Master Your Wedding Budget

Discussing money can be difficult. This is largely due to the money mindset we have developed over time, which can often date right back to our childhood. The things you see and hear as a child often stay with you in your subconscious mind as an adult. If you're finding it hard to talk about a large sum of money, then I completely sympathise, I really do. But let me be straight with you: it's important to set a budget and discuss an exact figure even if it makes you feel uncomfortable. We spoke about having a rough idea back in Chapter One, but it's time for us to get a lot more specific!

I've often heard couples say, *We don't have a budget*, or *We'll base our budget on what we find*. Big mistake. Everyone has a budget. Whether you're looking to spend £20,000, £200,000 or £200,000,000, everyone has a limit. There are three key reasons why you need to identify your budget at the start of wedding planning:

1. Be on the same page
Talking about money with your partner early on helps you understand where you both stand financially. If you can't get clear on finances, then you're going to struggle to move forward with anything else.

2. Have a clear starting point
A clear budget in place means you can start to work backwards and understand how much money you need to allocate to different areas of

your wedding. Without a budget, you'll be chasing everything under the sun, as there really will be no limit.

3. Eliminate time wasting

If you have no idea what you want to spend, then it's going to take you a very long time to pinpoint your venue or even your suppliers. The reason being, you'll keep searching for the "perfect one" when in reality nothing will ever tick all the boxes. If you go into wedding planning with this sort of mindset, then it will take you a lot longer to get things done than you ever imagined.

Here are some key questions you'll need to think about before setting your budget:

◊ Are you and your partner paying for the wedding yourselves or will you be receiving additional assistance from your parents or other family members?

◊ Are you saving up for anything other than your wedding right now, such as a house?

◊ How comfortable do you feel about spending the majority of your savings on a wedding?

◊ How much do you think your ideal wedding will cost?

◊ How much would you feel content spending right now?

◊ Do you have a buffer in place for any particular items?

So by now it's clear why you need to set a budget, along with the types of things you need to think about before setting your budget. The next step is to write down that magic number. You can write it at the front of this book, pop it on a Post-it or write it on your Trello board. I want you to think about this number every time you have a difficult wedding-related decision to make. At some stage you are going to want something even if your brain is telling you it's not a good idea. While a splurge here and there is totally valid on such a special day, you need to remember that overspending in one area means spending less in another. If you're not sure whether or not something is worth the extra cash, then just ask yourself the following question: does this align with my three things that matter most? Will this help me feel the way I want to on my wedding day? Will I still be able to stay within budget if I purchase this? If the answer to any of these is no, then you know what to do!

Remember, it's important to set aside an amount of money that *you* feel comfortable with, and both partners need to be respectful of each other's decision. Take Rishi and Selena as an example. It's clear his family can afford to spend more on the wedding than hers, but he is understanding of her financial constraints, which is important.

Now that you've got a figure in mind, it's time to dive in deeper and take a look at how to split this between your different wedding suppliers. Below is a breakdown of how much you should be spending on each supplier. As you can see, food and beverages are going to be your highest spend, followed by décor and then the venue.

Catering – 25%
Décor, lighting and florals – 15%
Venue – 10%
Entertainment – 10%
Wedding planner – 9%
Photography and videography – 8%
Cake – 5%
Transportation – 4%
Hair and make-up – 3%
Stationery – 5%
Officiant – 1%
Miscellaneous – 5%

Remember, the figures above aren't set in stone and are interchangeable. For example, if you fall in love with a beautiful venue that takes up 12% of your budget, then you can spend less on your décor. Or say you signed up to *Planned To Perfection*; you would no longer require a planner and may just want to have a coordinator on-site. This would cost nowhere near 9% of your budget, which means you'd have lots of extra money to spend elsewhere.

Keep your finances organised

Before you start making any payments it's essential that you have an efficient system in place to track your finances – and no, you don't need to be an accountant or financial whizz to stay on top of this.

I use a simple spreadsheet that logs the following:

◊ How much money my client is spending on each supplier in total.

◊ How much money my clients have left to spend overall.

◊ Any invoices that have been paid.

◊ Any invoices that are due at a later date.

I would also recommend a wedding budget Trello board for easy access, so you can look at spending on the go if need be. The great thing about this free app is that it easily links in with your calendar so you can stay on top of any payments due. If you're interested in learning more about how to use Trello to efficiently plan your wedding, then be sure to head over to my website at www. carriagesevents.co.uk

One question I often get asked about finances is: how do I actually save money on my wedding? I get it, you want something amazing, but you just don't want to break the bank in the process. There are a few simple insider hacks that I can suggest if you are looking to save a bit of cash:

1. Have a weekday wedding

Chances are your venue fee will be lower during the weekday simply because of supply and demand. What's more, venues will be more open to negotiation, as will other suppliers, as they're less likely to be fully booked on a weekday.

2. Full-day hire

It's common for most venues to offer a full-day hire only, even if you're just looking to have a half-day ceremony. It takes a lot of time for your suppliers to set up and dismantle, which means it will be impossible for a lot of venues to have another wedding on-site the same day. Some may offer you a slightly reduced rate for not using the entire eight to twelve hours for example, but it won't be anything too significant. So rather than split a civil and religious ceremony or an evening reception, it would make sense to have everything on one day so you can maximise the use of your space and get more value for your money.

3. Do your research before you attend wedding fairs

Though I'm not the biggest fan of physical wedding fairs (you can have access to hundreds of suppliers via Instagram alone), it's a great place to meet people and have a conversation in person, which will allow you to get a good feel for how they'll be on your wedding day. How do you save money here? Well, a lot of suppliers will have special offers on the day for any purchases made on the spot. If you've done your research beforehand and know your desired supplier will be exhibiting, go and give them a visit on the day to secure a good deal.

4. Double up on items

This can mean reusing your ceremony florals for your evening reception or doubling up your wedding favours as place cards. Hiring in chairs for your event? Make sure they match your multiple themes so they can be reused. You could also include some DIY elements; centrepieces and favours are quite commonly put together by brides. I'm not usually a fan of this strategy unless you have enough time to prep beforehand – the very last thing I want is my bride to be feeling stressed about boxing up favours during her wedding week.

5. Choose a nearby location

While destination weddings are all the craze (and I love them), if you're really looking to save some cash then choose a venue that is closer to home. You will save money on the fuel due to the reduced travel time and won't have to fork out extra money on overnight accommodation for yourself, immediate family members or local wedding suppliers.

These are just a few ideas on how to make your wedding budget go further, but I promise, if you get creative, you'll be able to find a whole lot more. Also, if you find that your budget changes along the way, then don't be alarmed. Most couples spend between twelve and eighteen months planning, during which time there could be changes to your living arrangements, job or anything else that could affect your finances. If you find yourself in a challenging situation, then it's often worth asking your suppliers if they would be happy to split their payments over a longer period. For example, with my one-to-one clients I tend to split my payments over four instalments. I know some other suppliers who do the same and some who simply ask for two payments. Whatever your situation and whatever your budget, I can assure you that you will be able to plan and execute a beautiful wedding.

Exercise:

1. Make a note of your overall budget.

2. Break this down according to how much you intend to spend on each supplier.

3. Put together a spreadsheet or system to track your finances.

The Added Confusion

December 2017
City Centre Hotel, London

'Winter weddings are so romantic, aren't they?' Selena said, gazing into Rishi's eyes, pulling him in close.

'You wouldn't have been saying that if you were here for the morning ceremony, welcoming the baraat outside.' He laughed.

He was right. That was the one major downfall of having a wedding in December. That and all the wet footprints that were currently covering the hotel lobby floor. The staff were doing a fine job wiping it down every so often, but the wet floor sign hardly added to the tasteful décor in the historic building. Selena looked around wanting to soak it all in. There was mulled wine and mince pies being served from a fake snow-covered cart in the corner, authentic carol singers in cloaks and a beautiful Christmas tree adorned with the prettiest handmade decorations she'd ever seen. Hina and Patrick weren't kidding when they said they were winter people! The smell of freshly roasted coffee tore her away from Rishi's arm and off she strolled to the other side of the room, waiting in line to be served at the busy coffee hut. Their group of friends hadn't yet arrived, and she didn't really know anyone else, which meant she had the joy of pretending not to listen in on the other conversations nearby.

'This is the most incredible wedding I've ever been to and the reception hasn't even started!' exclaimed girl number one.

'Look, they're even writing your names on the coffee cups like Starbucks – how cute is that?!' shrieked girl number two.

Selena leaned to her right to catch a glimpse. Wow, they were right. The coffee was being served in Christmas-themed cups and unlike Starbucks they were using metallic pens – how fancy! Of course, that was probably why the queue was moving so slowly, but the idea was novel, and she was gutted she hadn't thought of something like that for her wedding. All of a sudden, she felt a tight knot in her stomach. There was nothing extraordinary about their day. Nothing quirky. Nothing new. It was definitely not going to be talked about the way this wedding was. She fell into a daze thinking about everything she wasn't going to have, when out of nowhere someone grabbed her playfully by the waist.

'RISH! What are you doing?'

'I'm allowed to be affectionate towards my soon-to-be wife. Besides, I thought you might need a hand with those coffees.'

'I'm not sure you're the right person to help. Your track record with drinks at weddings isn't exactly great.' She chuckled.

'Ladies and gentlemen, please kindly make your way to the next room. We're ready to commence with the next part of the evening.' A middle-aged man wearing a large red coat was ushering guests to start moving through to take their seats. Selena hadn't booked a toastmaster for their wedding. She didn't personally feel the need, but funnily enough, this one felt like a perfect fit for the event. He looked just like Santa, but without the beard. She and Rishi grabbed their coffees and made their way inside.

As they walked through the doors, Selena's eyes twinkled with excitement. They seemed to have walked into some sort of romantic winter wonderland. There was fake snowfall placed tactically in every corner of the room, so that it wouldn't ruin the guests' outfits and hair. The bar was made out of wooden logs and decorated with stockings, mistletoe and ice sculptures. There was also an incredibly sweet smell coming from the back of the room which was filled with a row of huts serving tasty winter treats such as chestnuts, crepes and s'mores. Though they weren't quite ready to serve yet, Selena could only imagine the chaos they'd cause later on in the evening. There was no doubt about it: this reception was epic. Rishi took her hand as they walked towards their table.

'We decided we wanted something personal, remember? Don't freak out.'

She smiled. How was it that he could read her mind?

'I know you're right. I wouldn't mind talking to the chestnut guys though – that would be a nice touch for our drinks reception, don't you think?'

They both giggled as they took their seats, secretly feeling envious of the over-the-top event they knew they could never afford.

Chapter Seven

How To Stop Getting Distracted

Now you're clear on time management and have an idea of how to manage your budget, let's get into the next phase, which is a big hurdle that many couples seem to stumble over – *distractions!*

Have you ever looked at an Instagram profile and wondered how you got there? I've often found myself scrolling through someone's grid even though I don't know them. I bet you've done the same. If not, you might be on Pinterest, YouTube or a retail website... So trust me, I know all about distraction. It's so easy to scroll from one dress designer's page to another, and before you know it, a whole hour's gone by.

With access to multiple social media platforms, supplier websites, magazines, blogs, vlogs and more, it's super easy to get caught up in the whirlwind of picture-perfect weddings that drive up your expectations. While it's great to use all these platforms for your initial inspiration (we touched upon this earlier in the book), trawling through these platforms constantly will not only take up a lot of time, but will result in you feeling disheartened or confused. If you know your budget doesn't stretch to hiring a professional string quartet, don't keep watching videos of them. This will only get your spirits down. Instead, take positive action and put together a Spotify list for your drinks reception. Remember to focus on the solutions, not the problems!

Another thing to remember is that everyone loves talking about weddings, which means everyone will have an opinion on what you're doing. If you get too many people involved, you will find it harder to stay on track. It's absolutely normal to look to someone for advice but try and keep your inner circle small. The more people you ask, the more confused you'll get. And I'm not just talking about your friends and family here – I'm also talking about your suppliers. It's fine to ask your suppliers for suggestions if you're looking for other companies or if you want some feedback on the vendors you're thinking about booking, but don't ask every single supplier for a recommendation because you'll end up wasting a lot of time chasing quotes.

Speaking of supplier recommendations, once you've booked some-one, take that task firmly off your to-do list and move on to the next thing. I've worked with brides and grooms in the past who despite finalis-ing a décor company and paying a deposit were still adamant they wanted to look at other companies due to their own inner FOMO (Fear of Miss-ing Out). Wedding FOMO is legitimately a thing – but I know you're strong enough to fight it. Listen up, you've not just got gorgeous images clogging your social media feeds, but chances are you'll be invited to the wedding celebrations of close friends and family members, where you'll also be subject to a whole heap of inspiration. Remember, seeing someone else have something great doesn't make your event any less special!

I wrote about having a clear plan in place and this doesn't just relate to your budget. One of the biggest distractions *ever* is window shopping. Think about the last time you went to the supermarket without a list. How long did it take you to go around all the aisles to find what you were looking for? I can guarantee it probably took you double the amount of time (if not more), and you will have spent more money in the process, than when you took a list with you. Well, wedding shopping is the same. Whenever you go to a supplier meeting or a boutique, or even an exhibition, take a list of the items you need to purchase (or are looking for) with you. This doesn't mean that you're not allowed to look at anything that's not on this list, but make sure you start off with the essentials first, and then if you have time, visit anything else.

It's easy to lose sight of what you need and fall victim to the shiny-object syndrome as was the case with Rishi and Selena. When they attended a friend's wedding, they started to think about all of the great things they hadn't booked for their wedding and were worried it would set them back. Considering they were on a tight budget, there was no way they could incorporate everything they saw at another event into their own – and let's be honest, no one ever should! There is such a thing as overwhelming your guests. So now that we're clear on how to be as effective as possible, let's take a look at how we can secure the best quality suppliers.

Exercise:

1. Make a list of your biggest distractions so you can make a conscious effort to take control whenever you feel like you're getting sidetracked.

2. Remember to keep track of your to-do list somewhere: physical or digital. Once an item has been completed, tick it off, and promise me you will not continue searching for another supplier or keep going back to it.

3. Reread your "what matters most" list and also go through your wedding planning timetable. Once you see how much time it's already taking out of your schedule, chances are you won't be able to afford to get distracted.

The Supplier From Hell

February 2018
Rishi's flat, London

'We're paying him money. He shouldn't be the one dictating how our wedding should be run,' exclaimed Rishi.

Selena had never seen him this worked up. Things had finally been going to plan. The parents were all on board and in agreement, which was weird but nice. Everything was in budget and accounted for, and their wedding shopping trip to India in April was confirmed and booked. Of course, it was all too good to be true. She was a fool for thinking everything would run smoothly from here on in, which is why she wasn't surprised when they hit a new stumbling block. It seemed their photographer was being a pain for no apparent reason.

'Let's talk this through. We can get Tash on the line if it helps,' she reassured him, unfortunately seeing that it wasn't helping Rishi calm down.

'I'm not paying someone seven thousand pounds and then being told what to do by them!'

Things had been fine with their photographer up until this point. He came highly praised by a number of Rishi's cousins who had hired him to take their own wedding pictures. The portraits he'd captured were stunning, and he had lots of followers and likes on Instagram. Everything seemed to be in order, until he asked for a timeline of the day. Rishi and Selena were both adamant that they wanted to spend as much time with their guests on the day, without rushing around. It was going to be a long day. In order to save costs, they'd decided to have their Hindu ceremony in the morning, followed by a celebrant for their civil ceremony, which would then lead straight into an evening reception. This meant she'd have just two outfit changes and their guests wouldn't have to keep coming and going.

However, their photographer was adamant that the thirty minutes scheduled in for portrait shots was not enough and insisted on a clear hour and fifteen minutes, which was of course impossible when they had three events to squeeze in. While the couple explained they were happy with more natural shots, the photographer said his reputation was built on these shots and he'd never encountered a couple who didn't follow his lead. This didn't go down well with Rishi, who wasn't quite used to following anyone's lead – *aside from perhaps Selena's.* In short, they'd been going back and forth for two weeks with Rishi threatening to pull the plug on the contract if things weren't handled the way they wanted.

While Selena loved the photographer's style, she knew there were no winners in this instance. Their relationship with the photographer had already turned sour. It would be quite difficult to imagine him being the fun-loving, relaxed guy they'd encountered at their first meeting with him. And while she didn't want to terminate the contract and lose their initial deposit, she knew if they didn't genuinely vibe with the photographer on the day, the whole experience would be awkward and uncomfortable. Given Rishi's current state of mind, she didn't really want to make any outright suggestions, though she had secretly asked Tash to look into the availability of a few other photographers – ones she'd personally approached at the start of her search, before Rishi's cousins had convinced Mrs Mehta that this was the one they should be moving forward with.

Rishi flopped down on the sofa with his head in his hands.

'Now you know why his shots always look so great. He basically asks the bride and groom to spend half of their evening posing in front of the camera. That's not us – it just isn't!'

Chapter Eight

How To Find Quality Suppliers

Great suppliers are the backbone of any great event. You need them as much as they need you, so think of your suppliers as an extension of your wedding brigade. You'll be spending a lot of time with them over the next year (or two), so you'll want to ensure you're choosing people whom you genuinely like and get on with. I'm not trying to scare you here, but if you pick just one wrong supplier, it can have an incredibly devastating impact on the entire day – so please tread carefully.

In this section I'll be showing you the types of qualities a good supplier will have and share any warning signs that you should watch out for. We'll also look at where and how to find these great suppliers. One very important thing to remember is that you need to trust your suppliers – if you don't trust them, you will start to feel anxious and stressed as you get closer to the big day and will also spend a lot of unnecessary time cross-checking everything they're doing, which doesn't help anybody.

As a wedding planner and coordinator, I've worked with many different suppliers over the years (good and bad) at various different price points. As you know, I work with clients across the budget spectrum who are looking for a beautiful wedding with a relaxed vibe. My number-one goal is to make sure my couple and their families feel calm and happy so they can enjoy the big day. As a supplier myself, I will be open and honest and let my couples know if I have had a negative experience with a particular venue or a particular person if they're thinking about working with them – because my couples are my number-one priority. I don't take any kickbacks and I don't have a set list of suppliers I work with, which makes this outright honesty very easy for me.

Why am I telling you this? Because as a wedding planner my clients need to have the utmost trust in me – if they didn't, I wouldn't be able to do my job. This doesn't mean that everyone who ever speaks with me instantly builds a connection with me. That just isn't possible because we all have different personality traits – but it means that those who do work with me listen to me when I'm offering them some advice. If they didn't, our whole relationship would be difficult and a little awkward, to be honest. Whether it's your wedding planner, caterer or photographer, make sure you trust whomever you go on to hire otherwise you're not going to enjoy working with them.

Let's start by determining how you go about finding your suppliers in the first place:

1. Ask your friends and family

The best way to find a good supplier is through word of mouth. The reason being, your friends and family will never lie to you and will only suggest someone if they've had a good experience working with them. This is always a great place to start. Just remember that everyone has different taste and different expectations. If you know your friend or family member has a very different personality to you, then they may not be the best person to speak to.

> **Top tip:** Ask these people in person. Over the phone, via text or face-to-face will do, but avoid putting out a general message on your social media platforms. I often find that many responses on social media come from either the suppliers themselves or friends and family members of these suppliers. While they might be great at their job (we'll come to this part later on in the chapter), many who start responding do so for self-promotion and before you know it, you'll have a huge list of names to get through – so just be mindful.

2. Ask your suppliers

If you're lucky to have already booked one or two suppliers, then they will be more than happy to recommend others. While I would always advise that you vet these suppliers for yourself and don't just take someone's word they'll do a great job, most suppliers will not really recommend anyone unless they believe that they'll do a good job. It affects not only their own credibility, but it makes their job easier on the day if the overall team of suppliers is a great one. Please note some suppliers do receive a kickback for recommendations, so don't be alarmed if this is the case.

3. Keep an eye out at events

Chances are, at some point before your own wedding, you will be invited to another wedding or two. This is a great opportunity to check out suppliers. In fact, this is the number-one way to spot a great supplier. If you're happy with their delivery on the day, then that's a huge win. No matter how much research and how many testimonials you read, you will never truly know how someone is going to perform unless you see them in action, so if you do get any invitations ahead of your big day then be sure to RSVP with an instant yes.

4. Exhibitions

It's important to remember that anyone showcasing their work at an exhibition stand has paid to be there. They will be advertising their best side only. However, it's a good opportunity to talk to people and get up close and personal. I spoke about the importance of genuinely liking someone, and you can get a good (or bad) feeling about someone quite quickly when you meet them face-to-face. So, for this sole purpose alone I would suggest attending an exhibition or two.

5. Look online

Again, it's important to be careful when surfing the internet because you have to keep in mind that people will only show you what they want to be seen. But, as you're putting together your mood boards, you may come across some really great suppliers who match your style, and if you do, be sure to start adding them to your list. Look at their Instagram profile or blogs to check out other suppliers they may have worked with. This is a great way to research and find suppliers who suit your style.

Once you've found some vendors that you like the look of and are ready to start finalising contracts, there are a few things that can determine whether or not a supplier is going to be the right fit for you:

1. Do they understand what you want?

If you constantly feel like you're having to explain the same thing over and over again to a supplier, then they're probably not the right fit for you. Your supplier should be able to bring new ideas to the table that make you feel excited or should at least be in sync with your own vision.

2. Communication

What is their communication like? Do they respond to your emails and queries quite promptly or does it take them a long time to get back to you? If it takes them a while to respond while they're trying to secure a new sale, then more often than not, they'll take even longer to get back to you when they do get on board. You need to decide whether or not this is acceptable to you.

3. Read independent reviews

Whether it's on Facebook or Google, read independent reviews and testimonials away from supplier websites to determine the quality of service they deliver. It's also often handy to have a peek at the comments on their social media platforms, because if there is any form of negativity from a client, you'll spot it right away. Just be aware that the supplier may not be in the wrong – so look to see how they respond.

4. Ask questions

A great supplier will be willing to answer as many questions as you have before you sign on the dotted line. They will appreciate and value the money you are spending with them. If they seem like they're getting bored or frustrated, then you have to question whether you're going to feel comfortable asking your questions in the future. You want someone who's excited about working with you, not someone who sees you as a burden.

5. Look at their website

Be sure to also check out their website. The language they use will give you a clear understanding of their core values and the way they operate. How do they carry themselves? What is the overall aesthetic like? Remember, weddings are visually stunning events and you'll be able to get a great indication of someone's style and creativity by looking at their website. It may sound awful to read, but if you're not visually wowed by the aesthetic that represents the company then are you confident they'll be able to wow you on the day?

If you follow the tips above, then you'll be well on your way to securing that ultimate dream team you need for your fabulous wedding. Just remember that you will also be guided by your gut – listen to it.

Exercise:

1. Make a list of three suppliers to approach for each category. Be sure to list in order of preference.

2. Think about key questions to ask before any contracts are signed.

3. Remember to collate both online and offline reviews.

Part Three

The Finer Details

Congratulations on making it this far into the book. You've already hit many milestones along the way so you should feel very proud. This final section will really help you iron out the finer details and execute the vision that you have in mind.

First things first, we'll start by looking at venues and the types of things that you need to take into consideration when choosing yours. Every wedding planning decision you make will be impacted heavily by your venue, so this is definitely a section you don't want to skip. We'll then look at how to tie everything together – from your food and beverage, to the entertainment and décor. After that, we get down to business where I give you my top tips on putting together your wedding schedule – this is a MUST READ. Without an effective schedule your day will not run smoothly – you may want to find a highlighter for this part. And finally, we'll take a look at some of the things you should be doing the week of the wedding itself.

By the end of this section, you will feel confident and in control of the entire planning process.

Let's do this!

The Site Visit

March 2018
Rishi and Selena's wedding venue

The wedding date was getting closer, and though Rishi and Selena were feeling quite calm, all things considered, their parents, on the other hand, were beginning to fuss over every tiny detail. They were all due to travel to India next month and the soon-to-be married couple didn't want to wait until the final meeting to introduce them to their new venue coordinator. Both Rishi and Selena had been horrified to learn the initial venue coordinator they'd been liaising with had been replaced. This was the person they had entrusted with their entire day (aside from their friend, Tash). Her warmth, experience and support was what encouraged them to sign on the dotted line for the manor house, at what some would have described as a rather inflated price.

Heated discussions with the management had followed, and both Rishi and Selena had even privately enquired to see if their original coordinator would be willing to come back for the day for an additional fee – unfortunately it was against company policy. So, in a bid to meet them halfway, the owner agreed to personally be on-site during the event and even threw in some champagne for their wedding toast. Overall, it wasn't a bad deal, especially as her replacement, Tom, had been rather delightful. Though not experienced in Indian weddings, he was a charmer and eager to learn and please, which meant no question was too small or unwelcome.

Both families pulled their cars to the front of the entrance.

'Wow,' exclaimed Tash. 'It looked grand on Insta, but it's even better in real life!'

Selena beamed. Having her best friend by her side gave her some much-needed confidence that the day was going to be great. Though the parents were great, they were a completely different generation and didn't really understand how a modern wedding was organised – *well, her parents didn't at least.*

Selena watched as Rishi ran from his car to theirs, opening her mum's door first and then hers.

'Welcome to our manor, my lady.'

She took his hand, feeling a slight wobble in her feet as her heels hit the uneven gravel beneath her.

'Let's hope things go to plan this time,' she whispered in his ear as they walked ahead.

Tash was busy recording a video for her Instagram stories and the parents were still discussing the traffic they had encountered on the drive up.

Tom rushed outside, moving round the group, unexpectedly leaning in for a hug, which made Mrs Mehta take an awkward step back. Rishi, Selena and Tash couldn't help but giggle as they looked behind. This was going to be fun.

'Let's get you all inside and warmed up with a tea shall we? The owner, Mr Jennings, also wants to meet you all.' He took big, fast strides towards the door. 'Don't worry about the scaffolding that you can see on your right. It's just some regular maintenance work which will be completed before the start of wedding season.'

As they walked through the front door, Selena felt a flutter in her stomach. The place looked even more beautiful than she remembered. Tom gestured for them to take a seat in some rather expensive-looking armchairs and a three-seater sofa in front of the lit fireplace.

'Are you ready to run through the best day of your life?' He smiled.

Chapter Nine

How To Choose The Right Venue

As I mentioned previously, your venue really does set the tone for your wedding day. Location will determine whether or not guests need to stay overnight, access times will determine how fancy your production set-up can be, the capacity will determine how many people you can invite, and so on. So, don't take this decision lightly.

If you flick back to the budget breakdown then you'll know that the majority of your budget should not be spent on your wedding venue. Oh no, this should actually be kept aside for food and beverage. But, if you do fall in love with a stunner of a venue and feel you'd be able to reduce spend on your décor, then it is certainly worth considering.

Some of the key things you should be looking out for at your venue are:

Customer service

When you meet the wedding sales executive, or coordinator, how do they make you feel? Do they put you at ease or do they seem quite intimidating? Do they understand the type of ceremony or day you're after? Is there any room for flexibility? All these things matter because you will be liaising with them for over a year and if the venue isn't easy to work with, you're going to constantly feel like you're pulling teeth.

Time of year

Your actual date will be important when it comes to choosing your venue.

While some venues are absolutely stunning during the summer, they may not be very practical to get to in the winter. Narrow roads and uphill lanes in the middle of nowhere are certainly not ideal when there is heavy rainfall along with a risk of snow.

Capacity

When it comes to Indian and interfaith weddings, numbers can still be quite high. You're often looking at anything between 200–300 people, which is something not all independent venues and hotels can accommodate. Make sure there is plenty of breathing space for your guests and spill-out lounge areas. You don't want to be filling the rooms to the max and squeezing people in, which will only lead to guests feeling flustered and claustrophobic.

Layout

This links in very loosely to the point above, but it's useful to check the general flow of the venue and do a walk round from the perspective of a guest on the day. If you don't have exclusive use then you may find that your venue has certain restrictions in place for various spaces. Also, when conducting a walk through, keep an eye out for any great photography spots. Is there any outdoor space? Are there any beautiful features? These are all things to think about when it comes to the layout.

WiFi and phone signal

I have worked at a few venues where the WiFi or phone signal was almost non-existent. While this may feel like a blessing if you're going for an unplugged ceremony, it's quite stressful for your suppliers as they will find it hard to get hold of each other or their other colleagues. More so, you might find some guests feeling quite irritated if they're unable to book a taxi or check in with a loved one. When you do the initial site visit, be sure to check what the reception is like and ask if your guests and suppliers will have access to free WiFi if need be.

Caterer

Will you be opting for authentic cuisine on the day that requires an outside caterer? Not all venues allow outside catering and some may only allow you to work with a limited number of preferred caterers. Be sure to always check who these caterers are, and if they are suited to the type of service you require and of course work with your overall budget. You'll also want to check the kitchen facilities and cross-reference any rules and regulations when it comes to on-site cooking. Many venues don't allow a naked flame.

Lighting

You're going to need good lighting for various different reasons. First and foremost, without great lighting you might struggle to get great pictures. Natural lighting is always best, but if there's not a lot available, then check to see what sort of lighting there is in your ceremony room. Does it change colour? Are there dimmer switches, or do they just flick on and off? The lighting outside is just as important as the lighting inside. Is there any signage? If so, will your guests be able to read it? Will people know how to reach their cars when it's pitch-black outside?

Parking

Speaking of cars, parking is actually a very big deciding factor when it comes to venues. Firstly, you'll want to make sure there are a sufficient number of spaces. Secondly, are these a long distance from the venue itself? While this is fine on a summer's day, your guests might not be so forgiving if it's raining. Finally, if you're opting to get married in the middle of nowhere, is the car park basically just a field? If that's the case, it might be worth warning your guests, so they don't have to trawl through the grass in heels or in their newly shined shoes. Don't forget to ask your venue if guests can leave their cars overnight if they intend to get a taxi back home.

Other things to take into consideration are amenities: baby-changing facilities, disabled-accessible toilets, high chairs and so on. Is there sufficient storage for your items and changing rooms for your guests? It's easy to forget about the practicalities, but they really do make or break a great event.

I would 100 per cent advise that you put together a ready-made list of questions for any of your site visits to ensure you *don't miss a thing*. Make sure you've read any previous reviews from couples so you can flag up any questions based on these and be sure to check out their social media activity.

The following exercise will definitely help to put things into perspective, but I also don't want you to rule out that gut feeling. While it's extremely important to weigh up all the practicalities, you also need to keep a look out for those butterflies when you walk through a venue. Sometimes you just know it's the one and you'll be willing to make a sacrifice to secure it. There's nothing wrong with this – just make sure you're making the sacrifice with your eyes open and you know what you're missing out on.

Exercise:

Make a spreadsheet for all the venues that you've enquired about or visited. A list will make it far easier to compare them all in one go. Your columns should include:

◊   Location
◊   Distance from your home
◊   Price
◊   What's included in the contract
◊   What you love about the venue
◊   What you don't love about the venue
◊   Whether or not there is flexibility with catering

The Food Tasting

May 2018
Masala Magic Food Tasting Unit

'I don't mean to be rude, but I've literally had this same meal at every wedding I attended last year. We really need something more exciting!'

Rishi had been quite calm throughout most of the planning process. Well, at least up until the last few months. He'd let Selena call pretty much most of the shots. She had a better eye for visuals, given her line of work, was quite budget-savvy and understood the overall cultural requirements of an Indian wedding more than he did. The one thing Rishi excelled at though was recognising good food. His unhidden talent was the reason many of his friends would often call upon him for advice when looking for a new place to eat, so he felt extremely pressured into making sure the meal he would be serving at his own wedding was nothing short of phenomenal.

'Are we still sticking with a vegetarian-only offering?' asked the chef.

Rishi glanced over at Selena and met with her raised eyebrow. He understood what that meant.

'Yes, *unfortunately* we are,' he joked.

The two families had compromised *a lot* over the course of the year. The Chauhans had backed down on the choice of venue, while the Mehtas had agreed to a slimmed-down bar and serving no meat at any event. Though Rishi was initially opposed to the idea, it didn't take long for Selena to convince them that being vegetarian and vegan was definitely "on trend" and would probably go down well with his family's socialite friends and colleagues. The problem was, everything he'd seen from their caterer was pretty standard. They weren't reinventing any dishes or creating anything with a fusion twist; instead they suggested making over basic dishes like cooking the dal makhani with coconut cream.

'Rishi, we've been over the menu so many times,' said Selena, somewhat frustrated. She jumped in. 'Sudhir, the food you've cooked is delicious, but we are looking for something more fusion, more in sync with the Instagram links I sent you. For example, instead of a typical chaat, let's serve it up as a tart with fresh pastry and a tangy chutney on top. Our mains could be a fusion East-meets-West dish that's plated rather than served in bowls at the table. We have a small guest list, so it shouldn't be too difficult to ask people to choose their preference. We also need to ensure everything is vegan, with some gluten-free and nut-free choices.'

She took out her phone and started to scroll through her email to find the sample images. 'And I forgot to add, there are going to be some very well-connected guests attending, so if they like what they're eating, you're sure to secure some very big orders and lucrative deals.'

That last comment seemed to have caught the chef's interest. He perked up and started to make some notes.

'Give me thirty minutes. I'll get my staff to whip up some ideas while you wait.'

Rishi turned to Selena. 'Wow, I think you just did a "mum". Well done – she'd be proud.'

The truth is, the parents had been banned from the food tastings after their first attempt at attending one together. Everyone had incredibly different opinions and they did nothing but squabble for the whole two hours. So, Rishi and Selena agreed that until the final menu had been chosen and designed, the parents wouldn't be a part of it. But, with the wedding now only two months away, they were starting to wonder how long it would be before Masala Magic designed something they were happy with. As the chef hurried back into the kitchen, Selena's eyes met Rishi's.

'Well, we're paying them a hefty fee, so they better be wowing us!' he moaned.

Chapter Ten

How To Bring Your Wedding Theme To Life

Once you've decided on your venue you'll have a much clearer indication of the type of wedding theme that you can move forward with. Let's take a moment and go right back to your dreamy desires. Perhaps your venue aligns with this (great!), but perhaps it's a little different to what you imagined (totally okay!). Just because it's a little different doesn't mean you can't bring in elements from your mood boards. Just be mindful that whatever you choose should work with your venue. For example, your wedding isn't going to feel very vintage boho if you're getting married in a modern city-centre hotel.

In this chapter we're going to look at the other elements of the day and how you can utilise these to carry forward your theme or style. For the purpose of this section, I'm going to assume that you are using your "dreamy desires" and "most wanted" lists as constant reminders about what works and what doesn't.

The first big visual element of your day will be the décor. Décor is about more than just your colour. It's about the overall aesthetic of the day. There are three key elements that most couples tend to focus on (with everything else slotting in around these):

1. The ceremony area

Whether you're having a Hindu ceremony, South Indian ceremony or Persian ceremony, this particular area is going to play a big part of your day. The types of things you'll want to take into consideration are the types of chairs (do they need to be dressed?), the aisleway and of course the main ceremony itself. Inside the ceremony area you'll want to explore whether or not there'll be staging, what kind of seating you'll have and of course the type of mandap, canopy or backdrop, if you intend to have one. Lighting will also play a very key role here.

2. Florals

A good florist will often double up as a stylist and advise you on certain elements throughout the day. Whether you're looking for florals for your ceremony, your entranceway, aisleway or reception, most great weddings tend to include some sort of floral element, purely because they are the epitome of romance and beauty. Don't be alarmed if your initial quote from your florist is a couple of thousand pounds at the bare minimum. If it's out of your budget, just go back and be clear on what you are looking to spend and make one area really pop rather than trying to dilute the set-up across various rooms.

Top tip: You can reuse your ceremony florals for the evening if you're on a modest budget. It saves on cost and still ensures you're able to create that *wow* factor. Also, go with flowers that are local and in season to help with the budget side of things.

3. Tablescape

When I say tablescape most people automatically think about their centrepieces. Of course your centrepieces are incredibly important, and if you ask me, I'd personally advise you to go with centrepieces that are under fourteen inches or above twenty inches so that your guests are able to see each other on the table. Of course, if you're having a lot of speeches or any kind of video or photos playing on a screen set-up then lower centrepieces are preferable to ensure everyone in the room can see.

But, there's more to a great tablescape than just centrepieces. Think table linen, crockery, cutlery, charger plates and glassware. All of these items can be utilised to enhance the overall look that you want to achieve.

The next element to consider is food and drink. Between you and me, this is the secret to elevating your event to the next level. Seriously. How often have you been to an event and been mighty impressed with the décor to find once you take your seat at the table you're being served the regular curry, rice and dal? Food and drink is your opportunity to really bring your vision to life. For example, if you're having lots of greenery and want a very relaxed vibe, why not bring in a Thai element to your event? You can serve authentic alcohol and tasty dishes from the region, which really transports your guests to another place.

If Thai seems too risky for your guests, then choose a region of India. There are many different cuisines that you can bring to the forefront. How about a full South Indian meal or the taste of Gujarat? If you're keeping things Indian, then Indian wines and beers will go down a treat. The point is, your food and drink will play a pivotal role in bringing your desires to life!

Speaking of beverages, think about where they will be served from. Will they be behind a bar? If so, how will the bar look? Will there be tray service? Will waiters be attending to guests at tables? You need to consider what types of alcohol there will be, the garnishes, glassware and how everything will be presented. Not having alcohol? The same goes for soft drinks and mocktails. These are all things that need to be thought about carefully, rather than simply being left to the venue or your external bar company.

Finally, let's talk entertainment! While I love a great DJ at the end of the night, there are so many other things to potentially consider here. Whether you have traditional instrumentalists, vintage folk, or all-out indie rock, music will play a very important part in creating the right atmosphere. Even if you just need simple background music, there are so many choices. Do you go with Bollywood? Instrumental? Mainstream? Think about the kind of vibe you want to create and the different ages and tastes of those who'll be in attendance. I once attended a reception with my parents who couldn't wait to leave as the DJ was playing extremely loud rock music throughout the night – even during dinner!

But there really is more to entertainment than just your choice of music. If you're having a vibrant event, it's worth having some bartenders with flair to create some extra drama. If you want to encourage lots of interaction, then a close-up magician would be great. If you're simply looking for people to take some sort of keepsake back with them, then a photo booth with props, or a caricaturist might be a nice touch.

I know there's a lot to process with this section, but the number-one thing to take away is that every single thing you choose needs to relate back to your overall vision. Think about why it's there and why you need it. Don't just go for something because everyone else is. More often than not, they won't have gone into the level of detail that you've thought about because they probably haven't read through a book like this. You're already miles ahead!

Exercise

1. Think about the style or theme of your event and make a note of this.

2. What elements will you use to bring this theme to life?

3. Can you make your food and beverage menus more exciting?

The Wedding Handover

June 2018
Pizza Express, Manchester

Selena scoured through the menu, paying particular attention to the under-500-calories section, but decided her calorie quota might need to be utilised on alcohol instead.

'I'll just have the salad, please,' she said regretfully, as she handed the menu back to the waiter. Together with Tash and Rishi, she had been working incredibly hard to get all the wedding details finalised. It was as if the entire year had just flown by in a blur. Her life had been buzzing at 100 mph from the moment she and Rishi had returned from Santorini after the proposal. In between job hunting, wedding planning and packing for her big move to London, it was fair to say life had been pretty hectic. But at least they had Tash – she had been a godsend.

There was no doubt that Selena regretted not hiring a professional; someone she could have just offloaded everything onto. Completing all the paperwork had been a nightmare and though Tash had helped with chasing suppliers, putting together the Excel spreadsheets, and managing playlists, everything still had to be cross-checked. Nevertheless, they'd been working so closely together that Selena had complete faith that Tash would ensure the day ran smoothly. She just hoped there would be minimal interference from the families and was trying incredibly hard to hide her anxiety about it. She didn't want to cause any last-minute fights. It was definitely not out of the ordinary for someone to want to slip in an extra family photo, change a particular song or deliver an unexpected speech. She just hoped Tash would remember to stand firm.

'Well, we've done all the hard work. All that's left now is to make sure there are no hiccups – and Tash, that's your job.' Rishi raised his glass. 'To marrying the best woman in the world.'

'Aww, you're such a romantic,' Tash gushed. They clinked their glasses and took a sip.

Selena took a deep breath.

'This is just the beginning, Rish. I still need to try on my outfit, pack my last few boxes and hand-write all the favours!'

He took her hand and squeezed it tight.

'I know. And if you need me, I'll be by your side for all of that. We're in this together, remember?' he said, leaning in to give her a kiss on the cheek.

Before she knew it, Selena had tears streaming down her cheeks. This unusual outburst of emotions had become less unusual over the past few weeks. Everything seemed to make her cry, or worse, *moody*. She didn't know what was wrong with her, but she knew she had been a nightmare to deal with. Rishi raising a glass to her, despite her unreasonable demands and minor tantrums, made her feel like she didn't deserve him at all. She had been so busy clouding her mind with thoughts about the colour of the napkins and the size of the buttonholes, it had led her to pick fights with the one person who was the reason all of this was happening in the first place – *him*.

'I'm sorry. I've been such a nightmare,' Selena cried. 'It's been tough trying to juggle everything, and if it wasn't for the both of you, I probably would have had some sort of meltdown. Thank you for being my rocks. I love you both!'

'You two are getting far too sentimental for me. Can we get dessert now please?' Tash laughed.

Chapter Eleven

How To Put Together Your Wedding Schedule

You are at the final hurdle. This stage is fairly simple. All you need to do is put all your information down on paper, hand over the details to someone else and then breathe a sigh of relief. All the hard work is done, and you will be well on your way to enjoying the day of your dreams. If you've got a coordinator or friend on hand like Rishi and Selena did, then they'll take charge of your paperwork for you. If not, you'll probably want to grab yourself a highlighter or pen so you can underline exactly what you need to do. Throughout this book, I've mentioned a few things that can make or break your event, but let me tell you this: *no event will run well without a schedule, because no one will know what to do!*

When I work with my clients I do tend to go a little *OTT* in the sense that I usually have around twenty separate pages with me on the day at a bare minimum. The truth is, I like to go into lots of detail. If I were to hand over my documentation to someone who has never run an event in their life, they should not only be able to make sense of what's going on, but they should be able to run it successfully. You want your paperwork to be fault-proof so there is simply no room for error from anyone.

Here is a step-by-step breakdown of exactly what you'll need to include in your event schedule:

◊   Event date, time and location
◊   Number of people expected

◊   Point of contact at the venue

◊   Overview of all rooms in use, what they'll be used for and what time they'll be used

◊   All supplier arrival times and contact details

The above details can be listed on a separate cover page so you can have a quick glance if you need access to key bits of information. Following this, you'll need to go into your timings in great detail. This will literally be a step-by-step breakdown.

I would advise splitting the sheet into three columns: one to highlight times, one to highlight what will be happening at the given time, and one to list any side notes – yep, there are going to be a lot of details here. Here's an example of what we would write in each of these:

Time: 7am
What is happening: Décor company to arrive
Side note: All chairs and tables to be laid out as per floor plan by the venue staff

Another example might be:

Time: 3pm
What is happening: Bride and Groom to depart
Side note: Ensure make-up artist is in place to start working with the bride for her evening look

If you have particular people in charge of certain elements, such as walking you down the aisle or making an announcement, then be sure to add their names (and contact numbers in some cases) to the schedule. My main rule with the schedule is that *you can never have too much information*. Quite frankly, the more information you have, the less likely someone will be to come over and ask you a question. And the very last thing you want to be doing on your wedding day is to be discussing timings and details. You want to relax, enjoy the day, focus on the ceremony and spend time with your guests. Leave the rest to someone else.

Other must-haves that you'll need to include inside your wedding-schedule pack are:

Floor plans

Your floor plans should include a breakdown of every room that will be in use throughout your celebrations. Everything from where you serve your breakfast, to the ceremony, to the evening reception, needs to be included. You need to highlight if there will be any stages, how many chairs you want laid out per row, how many trestle tables will be required, where your guestbook will be placed and so on. Your floor plan needs to be detailed enough to enable someone who's never spoken to you about the day to follow it and lay out the room(s) exactly as you've envisioned (no pressure).

Seating plan

Most couples will usually have a seating-plan board or two displayed during their drinks reception, to guide guests to where they will be sitting once they enter the main room. If you have over 250 guests, then I would certainly recommend that you have two boards. Despite having the information on display, you'll often find there are certain guests who haven't found their names; they've probably spent the majority of the time at the bar, engaging in chat, or turned up late. Be sure to keep a regular printed copy of the table plan on hand for whoever is directing your guests. Remember, this copy will also need to highlight any dietary requirements or special assistance, if required. I usually have a team member at the entrance waiting with an alphabetical list so we can quickly locate names and direct guests to wherever they need to be seated.

Song lists

I cannot tell you the number of times I've been grateful for having extra copies of my song-list sheets. Most DJs are great, and they will have their system ready and set up according to your song choices. However, on the odd occasion I have come across some unprepared DJs who, despite receiving the information ahead of time, were not organised on the day, which meant having extra printed copies was incredibly helpful. You will need printed copies of your ceremony and evening reception music, along with a note of any specific songs and the exact version. There's nothing worse than starting your choreographed first dance and realising it's the wrong version – that would be an epic fail!

P.S. It's always worth making a note of any local taxi companies or end-of-night transportation arrangements on the DJ's sheet so he or she can make an announcement – particularly if your venue doesn't have a reception desk guests can turn to for help.

Just remember, if you fail to plan, then you're planning to fail (that's how the saying goes, right?). I'm not saying your wedding is going to be a big fail at all, but I am saying that if you plan and document everything correctly, then you are basically ninety per cent of the way there. The final ten per cent is very much down to the flow on the day and is often the reason why many brides do opt to have a professional coordinator. While it is an additional expense, it feels like a big risk not to have someone present when you've spent so much money on the day. Remember, just filling out all of the above paperwork isn't enough – you need to send it out to your suppliers two to four weeks ahead of the event date.

Exercise:

1. Start putting together a template for your wedding schedule. You can work on this from day one and keep amending it until a few weeks before. It's a useful way to ensure you're giving all your suppliers the correct information.

2. Look for free online tools to put together your floor plans so they have a more professional feel. A simple Google search will bring up various tools.

3. Start grouping your potential guests together early on in groups of 8, 10 or 12 so that you don't feel panicked when putting together your final seating plan closer to the time.

The Wedding Day

'Can someone please tell me where the production manager is? We need those vans moving right now to make way for the caterers!'

Tash hadn't quite realised what she'd let herself in for. This was a tough gig. She'd been awake since 4.30am, as she needed extra time to get ready. Not only did she need to report for duty at 6.30am as the wedding coordinator, but she was also the best friend of the bride, which meant she had to run the day in two-inch heels and a sequined outfit that weighed more than she did!

She was greeted with Tom's beaming smile as she arrived at the venue and breathed a sigh of relief as he took charge of her wedding kit and handed her a cup of hot coffee instead. Tash sank into an armchair in the drawing room and slipped off her heels for two minutes. She couldn't understand how all the planners in the movies wore heels – there was no way she was going to last in these till lunchtime, let alone the whole day! Once she'd had her caffeine fix and settled in the caterers, she rushed off to the bridal suite to find Selena and make sure she wasn't a nervous wreck.

'Knock, knock. Safe for me to come in?'

'YES,' called two voices from inside.

Tash tentatively pushed back the door and caught her breath as she stepped into the ridiculously large, light and airy suite. The velvet curtains were pushed back to reveal enormous windows which spanned from the floor to the ceiling, across the length of an entire wall. It was easy to see why this was the perfect room for a bride. The natural light that shone through was great for applying make-up and would be even better for her bridal photography shots which were due in fifty-five minutes.

'Oh my god! You look INCREDIBLE. Rishi is going to die when he sees you,' Tash giggled, giving Selena a quick peck on the cheek.

'Let's hope that's not literally the case,' said the make-up artist. 'Although you can't blame him – he's marrying a stunner, that's for sure.'

'I just came to get a quick glimpse of the bride. Call me if you need me. Wedding planning duty calls. I'll see you soon, my lovely.' Tash glided towards the door, blowing a kiss on her way out.

Selena's outfit was laid out on the four-poster bed behind her, ready to climb into as soon as her hair and make-up were done. She still had plenty of time, as she'd insisted on starting early to avoid having to rush. The day had started off smoothly, with Tom dropping by to deliver her breakfast in bed. Though brides at the manor were typically offered a full continental with a glass of champagne, Selena was treated to an exotic platter of fruit, which she washed down with a cup of tea due to her wedding day fast.

As she sat in her suite getting ready, she realised she felt calmer and happier than she had for months. It's as if all the stress and anxiety had melted away. There was nothing else to do now aside from simply enjoy the day. She really owed Tash big time, and already knew she had to return the favour for her best friend when she got married. As she drifted away in thought, her eyes glanced over to the bed where a shoebox caught her attention. She definitely didn't remember putting that there. She leaned in a little closer, while the artist was busy twisting her hair round the curler and saw a card balanced on the top of the box with the words: *For Selena.*

'Honey, could you look the other way please?' asked her make-up artist.

'Sure.'

'By the way that box you're looking at, I saw your friend leave it there before she left.'

'Oh, okay.'

As soon as she got the go-ahead, Selena jumped out of her chair and rushed over to see what was inside. She loved surprises, and like a child in a candy store grabbed the card to see what it could be. It read:

Dearest Selena,

Bumping into you two years ago was the best accident that ever happened to me. I know this past year hasn't been the easiest, but I wouldn't want to be on this rollercoaster journey with anyone else but you. I love you with all my heart and cannot wait to call you my wife. I know you never forgave me for ruining your favourite pair of shoes that first night we met, but hopefully you can accept my apology with these as we step into our new life together. Love, R x

As she opened and pulled back the layers of tissue paper, she uncovered a pair of Jimmy Choos that were identical to those she was wearing on the first night they met, except these had been inscribed with S&R on the soles. She smiled, knowing she was one incredibly lucky woman.

Chapter Twelve

What To Do During Your Wedding Week

By now you will have completed all the hard work, coped with stressful supplier searches, resolved any budgeting worries, managed external family pressures, and so on. All that's left for you to do is relax and breathe. You're about to kickstart your happily-ever-after with the love of your life, and while a beautiful journey awaits, do you really want to spend your last week running around like a headless chicken? No! Let's really break down what you should be doing in an ideal world…

There's no doubt that you may have some pre-wedding events on and if that's the case then you're sure to be tied up with these. Of course all the planning will have been done beforehand, but if there are any tiny tasks such as favours that need boxing or drinks that need dropping off then make sure you delegate these tasks to friends or family members. More often than not, people will be delighted to help. If you're feeling a little hesitant I completely understand. I find it incredibly difficult to ask people for help, but I always find myself feeling so much better when I do. Selena was the same. Her relationship with her best friend seemed a little strained because all her friend wanted to do was be there for her, while Selena didn't want to burden her. It's a typical case of miscommunication, but if you think right back to Part One of this book where I mentioned that people love to be involved – then you'll know that you're not only helping yourself, but you're helping them by letting them do something for you!

There are some things you can't delegate, like packing your bags. You might already be living with your partner, in which case there won't be so much to pack. If not, you've hopefully done the bulk of the packing or will be doing it at a later stage. It's certainly not advisable to be doing this in your wedding week. What you do need to pack, however, is your overnight wedding bag. Whether you're staying on location, or getting ready at home in the morning, there are some key essentials that you'll need. Be sure to download my bridal emergency kit checklist, but also remember to steam-iron your clothes, polish your shoes and make sure your jewellery has a sparkling shine.

Clothes and materials are one thing but you also need to take care of yourself. That means getting a good night's sleep, drinking plenty of water, and doing some sort of exercise or meditation practices to ensure you feel calm and energised. You want to keep both your mind and body in the best shape possible, as the wedding day can be quite demanding. This also means eating the right foods. If you've got celebrations taking place throughout the week, then it can't be helped, but try and avoid fried, sugary or processed foods, and avoid any excessive drinking. You don't want any unnecessary breakouts or bloating.

And finally, my number-one piece of advice that I really swear by is to spend time with your family and loved ones. This is precious time that you're not going to get back. Cherish it. Have some laughs, eat together, arrange the odd day trip, go through old photographs – feel good about where you are in life and about the direction it's heading in. Starting this new chapter of your life with gratitude will make it all the more beautiful.

You've done everything you can, simply sit back and enjoy the amazing day you so truly deserve.

Exercise:

Head over to carriagesevents.co.uk/plannedtoperfection to download your copy of the checklist.

Conclusion

Right at the start of this book I promised you I'd have your back every step of the way and I really hope that's been the case. There are many aspects that go into planning a wedding – it's a mixture of emotions, aspirations, beliefs and of course, logistics. I've tried to summarise these as best as I could, without overwhelming you, but if you ever feel like you could use a little more guidance then I would certainly love for you to connect with me on my socials. Whether you slide by to say a quick hello, drop a selfie with a copy of the book, or share your post-wedding snaps – I'd love to hear from you.

If you're looking for some structure, accountability and actual planning assistance, then I would absolutely love to welcome you inside my private members-only wedding planning community for Indian and interfaith brides – or better known as my brides' club! Inside this platform, not only will you hopefully go on to make some life-long friends, but you'll also be equipped with every single tool you could possibly need to master the wedding planning process. Trust me it's all in there, with regular updates taking place every single month. Plus, you'll also receive weekly coaching calls from me and monthly master classes from hand-picked experts. Simply head over to www.carriagesevents.co.uk to see if this would be the right fit for you.

On a serious note, I'm so grateful to you for choosing this book to be your wedding planning companion. I wrote it with the aim in mind of making your journey easier and more enjoyable, and hopefully that has been the case. While this book ends at your wedding day, the next chapter of your love story has really only just begun. Enjoy it, embrace it and make every moment count. If this is our last moment together then I want to once again congratulate you on having the patience and determination to work through all the exercises. Wishing you all the very best for your big day and all the adventures that await. Oh, and wait, you didn't think I'd let you go without a final word from Rishi and Selena, did you?

The Aisleway

Tash came bustling through the door barefoot with her hair dishevelled and her phone glued to her ear. She was completely owning her role as wedding planner with full integrity. She looked at Selena with a beaming smile spread across her face.

'Yes, we'll be down in ten,' she said, before zooming in on Selena with the camera lens on her iPhone. 'There is no way I'm letting you leave this room without a wedding day selfie.'

The two women giggled, standing in the bridal room alone. The make-up artist had left ten minutes ago to grab a coffee and the photographer was busy taking shots of the groom's entrance.

'It's your last five minutes as a Miss. How do you feel?'

'Strangely relaxed, thanks to you doing all the running around. We've been planning this for so long, I just want to enjoy it now.'

'And you totally should. Everything is running perfectly. I've called your uncles who are waiting by the door ready to walk you in. We're all set, my lovely!'

Tasha did a quick scan of Selena's outfit to make sure everything was set and not a single hair was out of place. The moment had arrived. Her best friend was about to marry the love of her life and though she could feel the tears welling up in her eyes, she knew her friend wouldn't be able to control her emotions if she started wailing like a baby. There was no way she was going to let that make-up slide off her face when she'd paid such a fortune for it.

'Right, they're waiting for you. Let's go,' Tash instructed.

Though the walk to the ballroom was only five minutes, it felt so much longer with the ten kilos Selena was carrying on her. The extra layers of net sewn on her skirt and the heavy jewellery made what should have been a stroll feel more like a workout. She made her way down the hallway as quickly as she could in her Jimmy Choos and saw both of her uncles waiting for her in front of the closed wooden doors that led to the ceremony room. They stood tall and smiled with pride, waiting to walk their niece down the aisle in true Indian tradition. It has always been customary for the maternal uncles of the bride to walk her into the mandap, and Selena was grateful that they were both by her side.

'You look beautiful, beta,' said uncle number one, while the second uncle took out a handkerchief to wipe the corner of his eyes.

'Okay, everyone, in two minutes I'm going to open these wooden doors with the help of Tom and as soon as you hear the music, I want you to come out from behind and walk in. Selena, when you get to the top of the mandap, your cousin will be waiting to help you take off your shoes.'

Tasha was doing her best to whisper, conscious of the fact the guests on the other side would be able to hear them. She quickly peeked inside and gave the priest her signal, after which he seemed to sing a few lines of something and welcomed in the bride.

The doors swung open. Taking a deep breath, Selena took her first step forward.

She felt sick and nervous, but happy and excited all at the same time. The photographer's flashing lights made everything seem white. She caught a glimpse of a few faces as she walked down and gave them a small nod and smile. She could see aunties whispering and friends weeping. Her uncles were holding her so tightly and pulling her forward, it was almost as if she was floating down the aisleway. As she reached up towards the foot of the mandap she could see Rishi's feet tapping against the carpet anxiously, his face covered by the white cloth held up in front of him. She kissed her uncles goodbye as her cousin reached down to untie her shoes and felt a gush of warmth run through her body.

This was it. It was her moment. It no longer felt strange or scary. It felt right. Everything about this moment felt right. As she glanced around the room, she saw it was filled with so much love and happiness and she couldn't have been more grateful. She instructed her cousin to take good care of the shoes and took her seat inside the mandap, opposite Rishi. As the white cloth came down she saw him mouth *wow* as he saw her. She smiled, looking straight into his eyes. Their relationship had come full circle and the day was going to be nothing short of perfect.

Epilogue

It had been two weeks since they'd returned from their honeymoon in Zanzibar. The clear waters, delicious food and incredible people had created a lasting impression, so much so that Selena had insisted they return every year for their anniversary. Rishi jokingly laughed it off, saying at this rate they'd be travelling all year round, as they were yet to visit a place that she didn't want to return to. This was actually very true and a lifestyle that Selena would happily welcome.

Instead, she was focusing on her post-wedding to-do list, which included unpacking, responding to congratulatory messages, sending out thank-you cards to all her guests, and preparing for a new job, which was due to start in a week. Though Rishi had been working extra hours to make up for all the time he'd missed at work, he made a point to have breakfast and dinner with her every day. Gone were the post-work drinks and in were the post-dinner dishes. They'd continued with their weekly date nights and he'd even started to show some interest in cooking. Sure, his dishes were disastrous, and Selena couldn't comprehend how someone could burn a basic pizza base, but she couldn't be happier – even if she was stuck with a shabby cook.

Her mum still had the post-wedding mother-of-the-bride glow and could not stop talking about all the compliments she'd been receiving from the relatives and friends who did make the cut on the guest list. *They said it was the most organised and lavish wedding they'd been to. Did you hear, beta?'* Selena loved the happiness it brought her mum and would be lying if she didn't swell with pride and gush every time she heard the compliments. Yes, her wedding was perfect and she knew it. She'd worked tirelessly along with Rishi and Tash to bring everything together and was just happy it all went off without a hitch. Even her in-laws had been singing the couple's praises. There were a few minor details the couple had conveniently forgotten to mention ahead of the big day, but once it came to it, no one batted an eyelid. Everyone was carefree and just enjoying the moment – though watching her mother-in-law trying to tackle a melting ice cream cone in the heat was a picture!

All in all, she was on cloud nine and still happily floating in the wedding bubble, secretly hoping it would never pop. Regardless, tonight was a special night. She'd planned a small surprise for Rishi upon his return from work to let him in on a little secret. You see, it turns out their honeymoon had been more special than they'd realised. The newly married Mr and Mrs Mehta were no longer just a couple – they were about to become a family of three.